the Timberline Review
ISSUE 10 | 2021

A publication of Willamette Writers

Editor-in-Chief	Maren Bradley Anderson
Executive Director	Jack Burgess
Associate Editor-in-Chief	Mohamed Asem
Fiction Editor	Rankin Johnson
Poetry Editor	Rebecca Smolen
Nonfiction Editor	Amelia Moriarty
Script Editor	Grant Rosenberg
Copyeditors	Dorian Hastings and Jacqueline Briggs
Proofreader	Asela Lee Kemper and Jaime Dunkle
Readers	Louise Barden
	Jacqueline Briggs
	Ellen Kozyra Currier
	Andrew Fort
	Asela Lee Kemper
	John Miller
	Stella Mortensen
	Debbie Mourey
	Daniel Pease
	Sarah Reichard
Cover Design	Lee Moyer
Interior Design	Vinnie Kinsella, Indigo: Editing, Design, and More

Editorial Correspondence: http://timberlinereview.com/contact/

Copyright 2021 Willamette Writers

ISBN Print 978-1-7320427-7-3
ISBN eBook 978-1-7320427-8-0

CONTENTS

LETTER FROM THE EDITOR
TIME CAPSULE | *Maren Bradley Anderson* 1

PROLOGUE
AN INCH OF TIME IS AN INCH OF GOLD | *Jiahui Wu, poem* 7

PART I
RAIN MOMENT | *Ashley Hay, poem* 11
THE MARROW-DEEP BITTERSWEET | *Mary Sweigert, nonfiction* 12
A NEW LANGUAGE | *Kate Gray, poem* 29
THE GREEN AGE | *Tobias Peterson, poem* 30
THE IMPORTANCE OF FREEDOM | *Kristin Bork, nonfiction* 31
CHILD OF THE MOUTH | *Laura Herbst, fiction* 37
FLIGHT 4590 | *Michael Hanner, poem* 45
PROM NIGHT, 1961 | *Jan Baross, fiction* 47

PART II
LOVERS | *Mallory Kellum, poem* 61
IN BETWEEN | *Susan Donnelly, poem* 62
LOUIS | *Hayley McCoy, nonfiction* 64
WHAT HISTORY MAKES OF US | *Marie Hartung, poem* 70
SUBTLE ARTS | *Billie Hudson, nonfiction* 72
FRIDAY MOUTH | *Jen Currin, poem* 80
OCEAN BIRD WOMAN | *Ciel Downing, nonfiction* 82
EVERY TIME I SEE THAT SPAM EMAIL | *Amy Miller, poem* 88
HOW TO BEHAVE IN SEWING | *Ruth Leibowitz, nonfiction* 90
COOKIE SEASON | *Sarah Mott, nonfiction* 92

PART III

MY GRANDMA'S ESSAY TO THE AMERICAN SCHOOL PEACE
    LEAGUE | *Suzy Harris, poem* 103

GREENIE | *Gabriel Granillo, fiction* 104

MOTHER'S LIFE LIST | *Stephanie Striffler, poem* 112

KELLY GREEN | *Robin E. Goldfin, script* 114

LOVE SONG | *Melody Wilson, poem* 125

THE SHADOW OF A DECISION | *Susan Field, fiction* 126

DREAM AS GYPSY MOTH | *Ace Englehart, poem* 136

ARTESIA, NEW MEXICO | *Celia Ruiz, nonfiction* 138

ELEGY FOR MY FATHER | *Dale Champlin, poem* 147

CONTRIBUTORS 149

TIME CAPSULE

Letter From the Editor

"Time Capsule," the theme for this issue of *the Timberline Review*, was chosen in August, 2020. It was dawning on us about then that our lives of isolation might go on much, much longer than we had hoped. I was a frayed nerve by August. So, "Time Capsule" was chosen partly from a desire to capture this weird year in words and partly so we could remember the other times when human interaction wasn't as constrained. As always, the authors of the pieces herein surprised us with the breadth and depth of their work.

Last year wasn't all about isolation, though. In June 2020, we at Willamette Writers "affirm[ed] our commitment to supporting everyone who writes in the face of hatred, particularly our communities of color, and those that hear and feel its sting on their bodies, minds, and hearts." At Willamette Writers, we believe in an equitable future. *The Timberline Review* is staffed entirely by volunteers from Willamette Writers—an organization that is committed to supporting writers from all communities, regardless of gender or sexual identity, ability, appearance, origin, religion, age, race, ethnicity, or class.

While we at *the Timberline Review* had already begun working on new ways to support diverse voices, we decided we needed to do much more. One step we made was to make submitting to *the Timberline Review* more accessible to BIPOC and LGBTQ+ authors in 2020, and we continue to explore more ways to diversify our literary community. We will also celebrate our past and present BIPOC and LGBTQ+ authors in a special part of *the Timberline Review* website. And while we are proud of the steps we have taken so far to make *the Timberline Review* more equitable and representative, we know we still have a lot of work to do.

As of this writing there is hope things will reopen this summer so we can see our friends and families again. We thank you for supporting this publication, and we pledge to keep working to make *the Timberline Review* a better literary journal, one worthy of all the artists between our covers and of you, our discerning readers.

Maren Bradley Anderson
Editor-in-Chief
July, 2021

DEDICATION

Thank you to the Willamette Writers Board of Directors for continuing to trust me with *the Timberline Review*. The staff of this journal is entirely made up of volunteers, including the editor-in-chief position. If you like what you see here and want to know how it is done, consider joining Willamette Writers and volunteering to work on the next issue of *the Timberline Review*.

PROLOGUE

AN INCH OF TIME IS AN INCH OF GOLD

Poem by Jiahui Wu

time used to wear thin
   but now it is going back to my mother's womb to hibernate
 another disappearing   into the green inapproachable mountains
mother's legs
        supporting a giant's mouth   swinging back and forth
   rocking
            like a yoyo before it stops
  mother said a good many things
                about things being different if I was a boy
I felt a boy inside
        saw nothing good about being woman
bleeding I broke my own
  hymen
        didn't want to lose it to a regret   mother said she wished
   she had another baby
 someone that turned out
               differently   I don't take it to heart now
  having another baby wouldn't have made any   difference to her
 (cheat her
we both pull
        down the blinds)
    now talking to my mother I do not   take offense   I do not
  expound on my take on life
 and she does not expound   on hers
      mother's time is limited   mine too is
why quibble over   what was lost?   it makes no difference if I was
   a   man or a
woman.
  or whatever I was

there are consequences   being
   an insect too   kills time
my mother my womb
I remember   lying next to you   my face pressed   against your belly
   listening   to the mechanics   of the working   of your intestines
   how sweetly
     you do not listen
too much
  remembering
worn thin
    remembering   I too can afford to   kill—
      remembering

PART I

RAIN MOMENT

Poem by Ashley Hay

you forget your place. especially your place in
this lush, blooming, sun-drenched world, which
has mountains and headlights and strangers on the horizon,
and also thumbprints and joyful tears and cicada songs.
and you forget that you inhabit a whole body—skin and blood!
flesh! bones! tiny crawling things in your stomach!
but which is a husk that often moves mindlessly through
this world as if it has lacunaed itself, emptily doing
what it has always done. and doing and doing and—
but then you stand under the rain, or in the fog, or

on asphalt somewhere terribly ugly, and for a moment,
rain kisses your forehead like a half-assed
baptism with no priest and only your bones as
parishioners, a skeletal attempt at divinity—
and you breathe in this holy attempt at undoing—
and you say to yourself, *this is the end of it all,
i am saved, O my lord*—only you are not saved at all,
simply viscerally, terribly aware of your own forgetting.
and of the rain. and of the headlights. and oh,
that is *something*.

THE MARROW-DEEP BITTERSWEET
THOUGHTS WHILE MOTHERING IN QUARANTINE

Nonfiction by Mary Sweigert

Spring

It hurts most in the shadows. The corners of their faces where I watch the cancelled everythings exacting their toll.

I already sense it's too early in this experience to be as tired as I am.

~~~~~

How telling—that lockdown life doesn't feel totally dissimilar to life with very young children. The isolation is real and reaches beyond physical distancing. It is a strange, instinct-driven experience.

~~~~~

The kids are like border collies. They need a job to do, constantly. Preferably one including heavy manual labor. They need to be kept busy and near exhaustion to have any hope of being tolerable to be around.

They get this from me.

~~~~~

We miss playgrounds the most.

~~~~~

If there is a rhythm to life in these circumstances, it escapes me. I grasp for the straws of connection. However slight or distant. I'm hollowed out realizing how profoundly I depend on visits from friends, family, grandparents.

How much others buoy my mother-spirit.

At least it is spring. Things are greening, and the breeze is cold but smells like nectar.

~~~~~

My natural anxiety settings are primed for this.

The weight of knowing it is just us.

Here.

In these four walls.

With no backup.

And precious few outlets.

I've taken to pacing.

I'm ashamed when I feel anything but despair or worry. Happiness, these days, must be a trick.

~~~~~

I cannot run enough miles, or eat enough chocolate. How can it think to be spring?

The audacity.

~~~~~

Sadness fills in all the gaps. Like sand poured into a container that already seems full.

There is always room for more.

~~~~~

These hard days are raw with loveliness. Every one of them.

First words and first reactions. Everywhere, reminders of things I would have missed. The surprise leg hugs. Yogurt smiles and peanut butter snuggles. The spontaneous Tuesday morning pancake celebration.

They are almost always eating.

They also get this from me.

~~~~~

I must find a place of authentic joy in it for myself, if I can ever hope to give it to them.

It is a harsh realization—that I have to change my thinking about, and around, this new reality.

Before my children completely combust.

~~~~~

Nothing ever prepares me for days like today. When you start *going going going talking answering getting fetching helping doing doing*

doing everything—but breathing—with bloodshot eyes and bone-tired muscles, well before dawn.

So we start the tank on empty, just hoping for a little miracle and not too much yelling.

~~~~

I look at her face in the evenings, after she has fallen asleep. Or stare at her school photo on my desk as I start the day's work at 8:15 p.m. I ache. It is physical and marrow deep. It is all the things that are classic anxiety: shortness of breath, a pit in my stomach, headache, muscle tension, carried in nearly every part of my body I'm consciously aware of.

But it is more than that, too.

I wake hyperventilating, as a matter of course. During the few precious hours of sleep found in these pandemic lockdown days. No stranger to insomnia, I find that this sleeplessness feels different. The feeling I could sleep, but first I must fix the entire world around me. What business do I have in sleeping when the Augean stable of our society needs mucking?

I know the privilege I bear. Because of which these worries are not more severe and perverse. That I only have to worry for our safety as soon as school begins again in the fall. Or as soon as I inevitably break down, unable to continue the work of the village with these two hands any longer.

I cannot piece together how we got here. I understand it. I witnessed it. I am guilty of not doing more to stop it. And I still cannot wrap my arms around the extent of the despair circulating in our lives.

I push it away. Guilty of that, too. Burying my head in the sand when the bravest thing is to stare, head up, unblinking, at what has become of this. Of us.

~~~~

Another humdinger. Exhaustion levels redlined all around and pushed onward.

The things we miss are carried heavily in front of us while the stress rides low around everything else.

Yet we are well. And well-fed. And the sun is shining kindly like it knows. There are plants in the ground.

~~~~

Being alone has never much bothered me. As a parent of little ones now, I crave it. Like oxygen.

Or ice cream.

Feeling alone is a different thing entirely. Feeling alone might be the motivation behind each and every self-destructive thing I've ever done.

Summer

Our lonely watch continues. Days where hours drag on the sweaty palms of our indifference. We should do something.

Anything.

So when we inch our improbably fatigued selves into bed, we might say we accomplished a thing. Yet even that asks too much of today.

And so many days.

~~~~~

Library days will save our souls.

We triumphantly collect new reading material from the curbside table, singing and dancing and skipping all the way home.

~~~~~

Migraine on a hair trigger—the price I pay for being awake. I pour my 4 p.m. coffee and wonder why I am perpetually jittery, yet I cannot focus on any one thing. My livelihood depends on the ability to focus—to string two coherent thoughts together. It takes everything I have to work this way and feels larger than life to sit down and do a thing. Complete a project. Send the email.

There is so much anger; I feel it in my veins. White-hot rage that will not be tempered.

The only thing that feels more like a real emotion now is the loneliness. The consuming depth of an isolation resulting from never actually being alone. From being constantly needed and hardly able to meet my own biological, emotional needs.

From wanting—needing—to take a long, slow inhale, only to have it catch before I can really start. With lungs that have shallowed themselves, atrophied, from ill use.

∼∼∼∼

I can write my way out of this. Think my way out of it. But we are moving upstream, always. Or struggling through sand.

∼∼∼∼

Nights are the worst. Or mornings. Or perhaps afternoons. Whenever looking forward to the next day is done most—that's when I feel it keenly.

Or when yet another late night tempers what hope I had for a better tomorrow.

∼∼∼∼

This time they are splashing in the bath. I hear joyful squeals of glee as they pour water over each other. The sound should bring only light and happiness to my soul. But instead, there is a weight. A crushing weight in the center of my chest.

Instead.

Instead of sharing in their joy. Instead of laughing along with them and bearing witness to the brilliant, fleeting moments of my children, I bury my head in my hands. Reading the latest email from school about what September will look like. How children will return to school during a pandemic.

How we will manage if they do.

And how we will manage if they do not.

∼∼∼∼

These early mornings. The obligations that go unpursued, for lack of energy. Or meaning. Or both. The list that lengthens with each day. I've no right to feel it as hard as I do. But it's tangible, this brand of anxiety.

Protesters being hauled off in unmarked vans is a tightly wound knot in my throat.

~~~~~

I love them so much it hurts. So much it takes my breath away.

And they love me back, big and hard and fierce. They know no other way about it.

I better start showing up for them.

~~~~~

It is a truth universally acknowledged that a child will always only ever want their parent's undivided attention.

Whether they are one or four or seventeen or thirty-five.

Even if they ask for it in wildly different ways.

~~~~~

Togetherness feels like its own weird poison, but sometimes the only cure as well. And we are together. How we are together.

Harder, sadder, lonelier, off-kilter-er, but together.

~~~~~

And what if I even learned something in this great slowing down?

I can feel some of it, the slowness, is good for me. Us.

Expanding into the happiness of small things. Learning how to sit with little pleasures and feel them all the way through to the end.

~~~~~

Worry for the kids is everything.

How going through these leaps and bounds without the foil of friends and loved ones will make its presence known.

Now and tomorrow.

~~~~~

We love each other. And that will always be enough.

Except when it isn't.

~~~~~

The swing set.

For the first time in three months. And oh. The joy. The terror-joy of it. Remembering the sensation must have come slower for the little one, but no less enthusiastically. The squeals of glee are medicine.

This reminder that light is there, at the end of a very long tunnel, bought me time.

~~~~~

Mild summer nights and looming moons, August is delight. The promise of fall. Not quite here, but close enough to allow a proper ringing out of all the joys of summer. Before the world shatters again, and the long dark comes.

But there is restlessness. In heart and mind and legs and breath. The realizations that there will be no brightly lit gyms to blow off steam, no cheerful gatherings to comfort this season.

We miss everyone and everything in this ever-lengthening drought of joy.

~~~~~

The girls smell like marigolds. They've spent the morning with me in the garden. I've always loved the scent of sun-warm marigolds. I love it even more, now. They peel back the petals to expose the rich black seeds and scatter them to the wind like confetti. Some are fed to the undiscerning dog.

Feet muddy, legs bruised and scratched and stained with raspberry juice, they pick cherry tomatoes in between flowers. You can watch for the exact moment the juices escape from the peels and into their mouths.

Grinning the way only young people can.

Everywhere I've lived, I've tried to keep plants. Ones you could eat, especially. It must have taken these years of struggle to get to this year's garden. It's modest, by most measures. But it brims with food.

Tomatoes reddening in the August heat, raspberries on thorny, shaggy vines. Basil. Beans. Fragrant lemon verbena. An embarrassment of squash. Carrots and bees, the odd pumpkin or two, and spiders and chives.

Pea vines have long since browned, yielding their real estate to Italian sweet peppers, ever so gently turning vermillion before our eyes. The lettuces are still, almost, hanging on. Just to spite the heat, I'm certain.

Walking out back to pick dinner has become my favorite time of day.

It is medicine, too, how gardens feel so rich and full of life. Even little ones. Even as leaves wilt or fruits rot on bad branches, the hum of growth carries on. They contain so much, sustain so much.

I've never understood why folks would use yards for grass. Not when you could grow other things—delicious, beautiful things. Lavender and cucumbers and thyme. Salal and rosemary and mint. It's reassuring just to look at. Not even that it's full of things to physically nourish, because what I think gardens are really full of is hope.

One day we'll move away, and I'll rest easy knowing those scrawny raspberry canes have carved out a proper patch along the fence. They'll proffer their plump ruby jewels to whoever comes after us on this chunk of dirt.

Maybe the blueberry bushes will inspire them to till and compost and plant in these raised beds we built and filled with love.

It's hope. Hope for the next season, the next day. The next generation.

I love you, little garden. Thank you for giving us more than I ever thought you could.

Fall

I can't stay here anymore. Under the orange skies, a smoke and ash headache crushing me. I reach for something to do that feels productive instead of futile. There is nothing to fill the void.

~~~~~

My reflex is to run. But there is nowhere to go. The smoke is racing everywhere. Choking off the exits.

~~~~~

We've lived in a city in crisis for months. Through riots and protests and pandemics. To have the skies permanently grayed over in the tangible wildfire grief of it all now feels like too much. Like it has to be the last straw. But in our hearts we know 2020 is young, and there is more struggle ahead. It's a staggering sensation, to realize this bottom could also fall out from under us.

Stress fatigue leaves me with no more left to give. No more money to relief organizations, no more motivation to homeschool, no more focus for my work. No more enjoyment for things that once spoke to me. I feel empty enough to drift out the cracks under the door. To join the rest of the echoes of dead things hanging over our heads, seeping into our lungs.

I'm just smoke myself, held together by decent intentions and deepening wrinkles.

~~~~~

The weight of this week has wrung me out. Between working and teaching and parenting and all the hats we now wear.

Choking on the worst air quality in the world. Cooped up inside, quietly losing our minds.

~~~~~

I had to leave the grocery store today. I started hyperventilating in my mask and couldn't stop. I abandoned a cartful of groceries, apologizing my way hoarse as I fled.

But we still need to eat.

~~~~~

These are the good old days. Even if I do a lousy job treating them as such.

I am here with them. Where we laugh and dance and sing and collapse from giggle exhaustion. Where we pour our love into art and meandering walks and Play-Doh and cookies. And where we look into the eyes of this gift of time together.

I love them in a way that proves I didn't really know how to love before I met them.

How could I have?

~~~~~

I can't peel myself from the floor. I see the world through a dense fog and everything is heavy, from my limbs to my children's emotions. I lie on the floor while the kids tear the house apart, eviscerating bookshelves and pantry cupboards.

That I am normally a person who cares about—needs—orderliness is of no consequence. I do not care.

Cannot care.

About the shoes in the kitchen, the so many pairs of shoes. Or the packages of instant oatmeal in the bathroom. I can't get off the floor for the weight of it. I don't even know what the weight is anymore, except there is so much of it.

My kids age and my hair grays in this state of complete and total apathy. It is at once my truest self and the biggest contradiction of my personality. We should be out basking in the few glory days of autumn. Instead—prone—I watch the world go by us. It is a gorgeous day. One of those sunny fall days where the leaves are sprightly and the sun is warm but the breeze is cool.

But even that is not enough motivation to get me to make lunch.

~~~~

I stutter. Things are perpetually half done. There are moments of manic energy and drive where I must start loads of laundry, finish all the work projects, wash all the dishes, straighten all the toys, sweep, vacuum, and answer those emails. I start, whipped into a frenzy of occupying myself. But just as quickly I lose steam and fall into the nothingness.

~~~~

A breakthrough moment—I interrupted a meltdown today.

I wanted to get angry. Felt it surging behind my eyeballs, but I managed to get out of my own garbage for half a second. Long enough to see the little girl who just needed some loving guidance instead of a pissed-off punisher. All she needs is my calm presence, my reassurance, my love. These things that are so easy to give.

Mostly.

I saw her.

Saw it is hard to share. She shares so much, so freely, I don't often credit her for it. I saw the storm coming, but it broke apart before landfall, and she was in my arms.

It worked, this being seen—*really* seen—by the people who matter most.

It might be everything.

~~~~~

Not realizing the way it might be interpreted, we took a full-moon walk on Halloween. A gentleman came out from a brightly lit house, masked and bearing a bucket of candy.

"Are you trick-or-treating?" he asked almost desperately. "We haven't had any tonight."

We hadn't planned or expected anything of the night, given the conditions of 2020, but happily obliged. He unloaded so much candy into the wagon we're probably set for the rest of the pandemic.

I know what he feels, what he expressed. I recognize it because it's mine, too. The desperation for even something small to feel normal again.

Instead, it's just two folks under the full moon, watching the flocks of geese tear through the sky, wondering what they know that we don't.

~~~~

There are days I'm sure I don't speak a word to them at normal volume. Because right away—5:15 a.m.—it's straight into screaming about toy dinosaurs, and I am hoarse by nine.

Other, better, days I am like putty. Filling in all the sharp corners and bouncing off the tension.

Soaking in all the delicious, fleeting littleness they have to offer.

That there are typically only these two mothers in quarantine is disturbing. Fate's twisted trick—that parenting requires our best selves, yet so often makes us a shadow of them in the process.

~~~~

I feel guilty for ever wanting space, room for myself.

So today we worked on art. I got out paints to show them something, a little bit of something, that makes me happy. That makes my soul glad to be earthbound for a few moments.

~~~~

In ten months of starving for it, I realize I crave being seen as a parent. As a mom. I need people to see me in the act. I need an audience some of the time, even if it's just my own mom or the neighbors down the block.

Really, it's the support, or maybe the leavening that happens when young kids are around someone who is not their biological parent. I live in the witnessing of my mom-ing, it recharges me. Gives me hope.

Instead of showering today, I wrote. Frivolous pursuits find few pandemic hours and minutes, so hygiene be damned, I wrote to rescue a vestige from a former routine. It's worth its weight in comfort these days.

~~~~

Parking lot spaces and covered faces. The days of cabin fever, counting our blessings, and crossing our fingers continue on.

~~~~

I read somewhere the strongest familial bonds are those between mother and daughter. So I should count myself doubly lucky. I do.

I know every good thing I manage to pour into them will come back out into the world again, multiplied.

Because that is the law of mathematics, and mothers.

A NEW LANGUAGE
AFTER "A NEW NATIONAL ANTHEM" BY ADA LIMON

Poem by Kate Gray

Ash falls white like bleached confetti, the woods raw
with screaming, the blow-torch of human carelessness
aimed at beetle-eaten pines and ravines. The only parade
is pickups racing home, then racing away, a bulldozer and forest-
service truck with twenty-year-olds, their smile-lines bright.

After 9 aircraft dump the Columbia River water on our homes,
after 800 firefighters, 6 bulldozers, after the wind dies down
somehow the next day, after 900 acres torch, after 30 dwellings
leveled, after 3 days, we return to our house standing, smoke, the sprinkler
wetting our deck, and Adirondack chairs our neighbors pulled away.

On the ground, bark pieces are charred blue-black from exploding
sap, oak leaves swept whole by the Gorge wind litter like
pamphlets dropped before bombs, written in a language we must
learn, a song in the throat of white oak that used to sing these hills.
A force bigger than us buckled our knees. Our fists rise in gratitude.

THE GREEN AGE

Poem by Tobias Peterson

Only after the fire: more fire, a biology
pushing through even to the last
which has been and is waiting here
beneath the table where once you promised
to drink me. *It's the end of the world
as we know it* and still the old labrador
lies at our feet and sighs into paws
while our talking grows heavy and bends

over him. The choked murmur of January
doves sifts through the stripped boughs and
means nothing apart from what it always has.
The day's green fuse is burning somewhere far
above us, low cloud and faithful gray muzzle,
above the dregs we raise to toast again.

THE IMPORTANCE OF FREEDOM

Nonfiction by Kristin Bork

Watch as the woman in the nebulous age zone, where she could be a hard-living twenty-five or a privileged forty-five, dresses in her green cargo pants, pink long-sleeved tunic, and bright blue headscarf; the same attire she wore when she flew in last night on the lightless helicopter that whomped over the heads of sleepy villages, industrious men as they buried IEDs, and furtive military operations that did not find those men.

Her right arm is a wavy curve from shoulder to elbow, more defined than the straight pipe of the left. She hefts a dull dust-colored Kevlar vest from the floor over her head and onto her torso in one fluid motion. The darker pink patches of the tunic, indicating months of sweat, slide neatly out of sight under the shield. She tilts forward and the vest moves enough to permit a gap where her hands smooth a Velcro belt over the round softness of her stomach. She stands and smooths the side belts around the back, so the heavy protection creates a flat field over her breasts and stomach, protects the meat and goo inside.

Steel-toed boots thud as she walks on the plywood floor to the foot of the bed where her red backpack glows against the rough brown wool blanket they issued her for the night. Hospitality for the civilian visitor to this small base, who needs to sign off on the commander's project before they can begin to build another school in a part of town where there is already a school that girls do not attend. She carefully places her helmet on her head, clicks the chinstrap, and holds it in place with the left hand as she tightens each side in turn, securing her scarf over her hair over her skull over her brain in a wish of metal to keep it all together if someone tries to blow them apart during today's walk.

Her heart thumps a bit. Eight months in, she is still waiting for the day it won't thump under her ribs as she grasps the rough edge of the Velcro embroidered patch that lists her last name, agency, and blood type, and unsticks the Velcro enough to hook it onto the front of her vest. Should she have the misfortune to feel the unrelenting boom and shriek of shrapnel or worse, this small Velcro patch will tell the field medics what blood she needs as she lies in the possibility of bleeding out.

Cold black steel and thick sturdy webbing of two tourniquets are next. One in a holder on the upper left of her chest, over her heart, where her hand goes when she meets school officials and health clinic leaders and lowers her eyes in respect and murmurs, "*Wa'alaykum as-salam,*" in response to their greeting. She slips the other tourniquet into the pocket of the right thigh of her cargo pants. Kitty-corner tourniquets so that regardless of which leg or arm has been shot or blown off, there is a good chance of having a way to keep as much blood as possible inside.

The sun is bright against a limitless blue sky as she steps out from the container to join the gaggle of boys dressed in dung-colored pants and shirts, small guns glinting in holsters at their waists and the large guns are black slashes over their shoulders or cradled in their arms.

Note the impact the lone pink-and-blue body makes against the bodies clothed in pixels of mud and dust and dull green that this group makes against the sky.

A slight heated breeze dances with the wisps of blond hair that escape the confines of her headscarf and helmet. She doesn't shellac her hair into place the way the girls who carry guns do, the few girls. The conversation of the boys lags and softens as they witness this controlled chaos. Does it make them miss home?

Six of the boys with guns walk toward the woman. One steps forward, the tallest one who might not still be a boy, but they are all boys with guns. "We will follow this path." He gestures to a chalkboard where their route through town has been drawn in a series of X's and O's and lines and squares. Her eyes go glassy and inattentive. Minutes and paragraphs later, the tallest one says, "Let's go."

She notes the muffled thump of fourteen boots on dirt as the seven walk out of the gates that demarcate what is inside the wire and outside the wire, inside of safety and outside of safety, and they head up the middle of the street bordered by the tan walled courtyards of the neighborhood. Two of the boys with guns engage in easy conversation with the woman, ask where she is from and how long she has been in-country and where else in-country she has been. She tells them about KAF (Kandahar Airfield) and the TGI Friday's where they sing "Happy Birthday," and their fluorescent drinks have no alcohol to make a TGI Friday's in the middle of Afghanistan; and dry raves; and PXs run by the different countries there, especially the German one with the largest selection of knives and the most alarming T-shirts commemorating the war. The boys with guns tease her over their jealousy of hamburgers and lattes and donuts.

There's a sudden slap of many feet against the dusty street. A cluster of schoolboys with small cloth bags rush up to the rotating cast of boys with guns. The schoolboys under age eleven have never known a day when some boys with guns and strange exoskeletons did not live in the fortress at the edge of town. "Hello! Give me a pen!"

The woman searches her bag for the packet of pencils. Her helmet slips a bit over her forehead, shades her eyes and dislodges the blue headscarf underneath. She offers a pencil and a toothy smile to the short schoolboy dressed in blue cap and shalwar kameez. She has not seen a child in six months. The short schoolboy smiles close-lipped and accepts it, then hands it to the tall schoolboy in burgundy as more schoolboys surge forward in a flurry of greens and golds and browns to claim their pencils. Soon, the woman has no more pencils and stands to the side and watches while the boys with guns' pockets empty of candy.

Schoolboys laugh and scream around the sweet redness of the mouthfuls of hard candy, "Give me a pen! What is your name?" as they race along the dust-colored wall toward a narrow gate and disappear inside.

The boys with guns and the woman walk at a pace suggesting ease down the middle of the street to visit a school located just past the outdoor market. Americans rebuild and rebuild schools and clinics and markets to strengthen the town's faith in the national government. Schools here are awash in the cool blue and industrial green paints left over from the days of the Soviets. Remnants reminded her of stories she'd heard of the war before that helped to create the conditions for this one. Inside the main hallway of every school she visits is a hand-painted sign that proclaims this building a gift from the American people, an awkward pair of painted hands clasp each other in friendship. She makes a hollow bet with herself for a secret beer when she gets back to her own bed that this trend will hold true, the hands of the Americans will stretch across the ocean here as well.

She doesn't think the American people remember offering such a gift.

Tart, sharp pomegranate and freshly butchered meat smells mingle in the air. Men stand, sit, crouch as they chatter and laugh next to their wares on folding tables under the dappled shade of striped, faded textiles at the open-air market next to the school.

The group of boys with guns and the woman continue toward the school past the market as a man drives a small rusted green LADA toward the group of boys with guns with the nonchalance of a man who has watched these guns move around his town with impunity for what may be at this moment just long enough to become unbearable.

Prickles of panic start in the woman's stomach and branch and curl into thin vines through her arms to the tips of her fingers and down her legs to her feet and up her neck until her head feels cool under the sweaty confines of her helmet as she realizes the man does not plan to stop his slow, easy drive directly into them and their path of safety in the middle of the street away from houses and gates where dangers remain more easily hidden.

The boys with guns move with swift smooth formation into position with the woman in the center back, and the boy with the largest gun and loudest voice moves to the front.

A bellow that strives for commanding highlights his fear: "Stop your fucking car! Stop now!"

He swings his gun from the casual cradle of his arms to point at the head of the man behind the windshield.

The conversations at the market stop.

The shouts of a frightened boy with a gun echo in the street as he stands between his group of boys with guns drawn in front of the woman in a blue headscarf that matches her eyes on silent tiptoe peeking over the wall of shoulders and a rusted rumbling green LADA driven by a middle-aged man with a beard who just wants to take home meat for his family's evening meal.

The tall boy with a gun rams his booted right foot into the hood of the car and screams at the man behind the windshield who raises his hands, then lowers them to cover the bones of his neck with the bones of his fingers as he bows his head forward.

Wonder if he wishes he had made a different choice.

The confusion on his face may indicate that he is unsure which choice made that day, that week, that life, was wrong.

The woman tries to see around the boys with guns who make a wall of shoulders in front of her. Balanced on her tiptoes, core held tight so that she does not grip their tense backs for support, she watches the scene. Her face is blank, eyes that squinted a second ago smooth and widen, brow furrows up into the lip of the helmet as she watches.

Muffled sounds coming from the man with his fingers over his bowed neck bounce off the windshield and vibrate around the interior of the car, only the feeling of placating speech tinged with anger makes it outside. He speaks Pashto and the boys with guns know only the greeting words in Pashto. A terp didn't come on today's walk. The lead boy with a gun pushes again on the hood of the car with his booted foot and motions with his rifle. "Back the fuck up!" Without a glance ahead at the gun, the man stares without seeing the wheel he places a hand upon and backs up into the plume of dust his car grinds up, past the market. Reverses into the next road. The growl of the car grows fainter.

The lead boy and one at each flank walk forward to check the street the car backed into, point their guns this way and that at the silent crowd of market men who have tables of fruit and meat to sell before the end of the day. Three boys with guns remain behind to watch from the back and keep the woman in place until the area is secure. Her tiptoe perch does not waver, her eyes stay wide. The Kevlar vest moves up and down with intentional breath.

A gun motion from the lead boy with a gun releases the wall of shoulders and the group moves into the market, errand at the school forgotten. A brief break and bit of normalcy before they head to the school for a visit and hopeful approval for a new one to be built. The commander is only in-country for another few months and needs a project completed. The market men shake their shoulders and start to chatter again, some light cigarettes. They greet the boys with guns who brought money to haggle over pomegranates and cigarettes and bootleg DVDs.

The woman speaks to no one and accepts no pomegranates that the lead boy with a gun offers her.

CHILD OF THE MOUTH

Fiction by Laura Herbst

It's my first night in Mobenga, where cliff rocks feel like teeth under my feet. Where words ping, and the Sahara spits sand in my eyes. I'm twelve and don't know what a clap-clap-clap in the middle of the night might mean. But it wakes me up, this clap-clap-clap, moonlight glimmering through the tent window, my tongue scratching in my mouth. Gritty bits of desert coat the sleeping bag, and my ponytail feels sandpapery and strange in my hand. Clap-clap-clap, I hear again. I sit up. My head brushes the top of the mosquito net. The wind's quiet.

What I know: The bush man with the shriveled leg told me yesterday—don't be afraid of *nyobig*, who roams at night, rooting for leftovers like a pig. But maybe the crocodile would consider me a leftover. Hah!

What else I know: It's 1983, the Bible has sixty-six books and Uncle would have me read all of them. The four of us—Uncle Taft, Aunt Melba, my cousin Hank and me—arrived in Togo two weeks ago. Then, we took taxis and a helicopter to the bush country, arriving yesterday. Course, I miss Mama. She died back in North Carolina, and Uncle says it was the curse of God got her because she didn't pray. Now we're in Mobenga, and Uncle wears crosses around his neck, and he says to call the folks here "bush people" because they're not Saved until they give up their stories, pouches, and bottles of good luck.

Also: The bush man's name starts with *Kuh*, and I forget how to say the rest of it. The first Benga words he taught me as we sat under the mango tree were not *Mama* and *Daddy*, not *sister* and *brother*, but *nyo* meaning mouth, *big* meaning child, and *nyobig* meaning crocodile, a child of the mouth, a name of a wild, unknown thing. *Nyobig*, I think. *Nyobig*, I say, wheezing the words out of my dry, dirt-coated throat.

Clap-clap-clap—and a smell like the green on a pond seeps through the window. Silence settles like a breath at the back of my neck.

I slip out from under the mosquito net, the ground hard under my knees. I don't call for Aunt and Uncle; they wouldn't know what to do. I'm the one closest to the footpath. Aunt Melba and Uncle Taft are yards away in their tent, and Hank's in his own tent, too. I unzip the door flap and peek through the opening; the dust gathered at the door powders my face. I imagine that wide mouth opening with its jagged teeth, the nearly white gums, the fuchsia-pink tunnel that becomes seemingly endless. I have the lantern in my hand, ready to thrust it down his throat. Hah!

But against the violet sky (Mama told me to say *violet*, not *purple*), I see a woman's silhouette. She's wrestling with something in her arms, and she's running toward me, the stripes of her *pagne* coming into view.

"*Si…vous…plait*," the woman calls to me, in French that's as broken as mine. "My baby…sick." She's leaning over now. On her forehead a scarf is tied in a bow, in the style of the bush women. A sliver of moon hovers over her head.

Peeking out of the tent, I can smell the dirt that clings to all of our legs. "A minute," I croak in French, unable to think of any of those Benga words *Kuh* taught me. I turn and rummage in the tent for my sandals and the matches. Fumbling with the lantern, I light the wick and stick the box of matches in my panties. Then, I stand up, outside, pulling my tank shirt long, over my *derrière*, as I'm trying to learn to say because the people here speak French or Benga.

The lantern lights the woman's sweaty skin and the baby in her arms, its legs stiff as boards. This woman's face isn't marked with the knife slashes like *Kuh*'s sister, who brought us water, who showed us how to scoop the water with calabashes, the muck undisturbed at the bottom.

This woman is tall, thin, her face sunken like a raisin, sunken under the weight of…the baby wails. Green goo runs down the woman's arms, and the whiff of the baby stinks. And now Uncle and Aunt are beside me, their breaths sounding through their mouths like little winds. Aunt's in curlers and a net, and she's tying the belt of a pink terry cloth robe that seems too thick in Mobenga's gritty heat. Uncle's in cut-off sweatpants, his bony knees are bruised and dirty from kneeling on the ground, and his hair is tousled as if it's about to slip off his head. I hear Hank coughing in his tent.

The woman twirls her finger to show a whirling motion. "*L'hôpital*," she says. "Take my baby up."

I swallow and translate. "She wants the helicopter. She wants us to take her baby to the hospital. In Dapaong, right?"

Silence. Above, the clouds move and darken the moon, the stars. I can't take my eyes off the baby's rigid legs.

"I'll get the first aid kit," Aunt Melba says. Her plastic thongs flap as she takes my lantern and goes back to the supply tent where they've slept.

Uncle Taft shuts off his flashlight. He raises his hand above his head, as though he's testing the fruit in God's hanging garden. He doesn't look at the bush woman, and I realize he's not going to radio for the helicopter. Instead, he whispers in my ear: "What we do doesn't matter," he says, his fingers fluttering above me. "What He does means everything."

Aunt Melba comes back and opens the case; I hold the lantern so she can see. She selects a jar of petroleum jelly. "We're going to pray to Jesus to help her baby."

More green pours out of the baby's bottom. More cries echo off the distant rocks. My knees go soft. The night feels warm, everything warm.

My aunt makes wiping motions with a sponge and gives the gauze to the woman. She pops open the jar of petroleum jelly, and the bush woman grabs it, rubs the salve on her baby, a girl, until the chest, arms and neck are covered in a shiny film. The mother's forehead creases, the two of them sweating in the lantern's light. Above, the clouds move again, and I can see that sliver of moon.

Uncle bows his head and closes his eyes, and he says more loudly, "Lord Jesus, sitting there on your golden throne, I come before you with a heart so burdened I can hardly bring myself to speak Thy Holy Name." He sucks in a wad of air and continues. "We are humble sinners ourselves, here among heathens. Why do the bush people imagine a vain thing?" He points to the baobabs; the gnarled branches form a silhouette against the night sky. "Because they have not yet heard the wonder of the Word," Uncle continues. "For without the Message, we are nothing but heathens."

"Thank you, Jesus," Aunt says. "Bring this baby into the Light."

But the baby convulses with such force she almost jumps out of her mother's arms. Those baby legs curl, then straighten, curl and straighten again—and the woman scrambles to keep the baby in her arms.

Uncle and Aunt tell me to get back in my tent, then amble back to theirs, the ray of their flashlight shivering from low batteries. The murmurings are faint.

"As if we…every sick person," Aunt says.

"Remember why…we're on a budget," Uncle says.

The woman lets out a cry and throws down the jar of petroleum jelly, which thuds into the sand at my feet. She slips the baby onto her back, tucks the body into the folds of her *pagne*—and she marches into the shadowy field. Now, the baby is quiet. I can hear the woman's feet pad the soft, worn dirt of the path. No air conditioner hums, no television drones, no car screeches in the distance. I'm standing with the lantern in my hand, and when it sputters out, the stars come low over me. I wish I'd brought those pictures hidden under the sweaters back home—pictures of Mama holding me as a baby, the waves of her hair falling over me like curtains, like this African night.

I follow the bush woman. I can give her my lantern, the matches. But she doesn't need it, even I can tell that. The shard of moon shines, making the path a silvery wisp in the bluish field and ahead the huts look black. I creep through the field. The cut millet stalks scrape my bare calves. The lantern bumps against my knee.

"*Attendez*," I call out. I'm not sure what I'll say to her. I don't know how to get the helicopter. Or to say the petroleum jelly is no good, that our God is fickle, our magic fallible. And that we have no money, even though we're white. How to tell this woman I've watched the devout fall on the ground, speak in tongues, eyes rolling, spit drooling? I know the hymns, the prayers, the swoons, the fan spinning over the heads of the sweat-drenched choir. But sometimes I think the unlucky have each other and that's all.

I tell myself she's a bush woman—she's used to suffering. Isn't that what the chief said yesterday as his men led the moaning pregnant woman away—*nos femmes souffrent*? I keep on, following the baby's stink. Above, the night sky seems forever.

She stops at one of the huts. Clap, I hear again. Clap-clap-clap. Now I remember there are no doors in Mobenga, just holes in walls, and people clap when they want someone to come out of the hole. Someone comes to the entrance. Voices whisper. Coins flash in her hand. Maybe the baby is safe now. I stop, crouch down, wishing Mama were here. She'd know what to say.

But the bush woman is off again and turns toward the cliffs. She paces along the edge—her head bobs up and down the escarpment's razored line. I follow, the lantern swinging in my sweaty hand. I can still give it to her. I've got the box of matches stuck in my underwear. Because I'm thinking she might march all the way to Dapaong herself. Seventeen miles through the bush, Uncle's told me. She's not giving up. Hah!

I stumble over the points of rocks, the roots of trees, rushing to the lip of the cliff. Below, the woman's picking her way down the rocks, the baby a quiet lump on her back, and she disappears into the dark throat of the night.

"*A gúúl,*" I call out, remembering now a Benga word. I reach with my unlit lantern as if I might drop it to her. As if I'm like those stars that hang close and beautiful but can do nothing to help. As if the mouth of the crocodile I see among the stars is about to snap, and we can stop it.

Weeks later, I'm sitting before a fire, and I've learned to say Kombaté's name and that his leg shrunk after French missionaries stuck a needle too far into his ass. That's what he says anyway, and he uses the word *ass*, which I taught him. He also knows *shit* and *damn it*. Right now

I'm telling his sister, who fetches our water, how the sky looked like *nyobig*, his big, open mouth. We make hand gestures, mix French and Benga. Her face is shimmering, orange in the firelight. "*A nyobig*," she laughs, making a long beard with the smoke that comes off the fire. She shows me how to grab the smoke and make it hang for a moment off my chin, like *nyobig*'s snout.

I'm making a child of the mouth, and I tell her the story. How the baby shook its legs, got quiet. How I followed them through the field and watched them go down into the night. The smoke warms my chin and rises up. I tell her how the stars formed an outline of *nyobig*'s mouth and his twinkling teeth.

She listens and rubs her teeth with a stick of *neybiele*. "The baby died," she says. "There was nothing to do." She waves the smoke away, as if the bush people expect nothing of us now. They don't expect our prayers to work. They don't expect us to solve their problems. They don't expect us to share our supplies or even to dynamite that well we promised. They expect *yán*. Nothing. But they do like a story.

As the long plume of smoke creeps up my chin, I want to be useful somehow, to find a way to belong the way this bush woman does, the way she slips the knot off her waist and upends the gourd, swallowing its contents. The way she clicks her tongue and urges me to press the gourd to my lips. The firelight wets her face.

"Bee-bah-bay," she tells me, pronouncing slowly, correcting my pronunciation. "Call me Bibabé."

I shake my head because Uncle has told me not to drink their drink or eat their food. Parasites, he's warned.

She shrugs her shoulders. She pours a little *tchakpa* on the ground—for the ancestors, she says. And the ground foams and sizzles. "Talking ancestors," she laughs, takes a drink, waves the smoke my way.

And I believe her. I tilt one ear over the frothing ground, and I want to clap-clap-clap for Mama to come out of her hole.

Sometimes during the day I climb down to the crocodile pond, which is at the bottom of the rocky cliff, where the women fetch their water. These days are bright, with a scalding sun, and the women gather around the pond, wrapped in their cocoons of cloth yellowed by the Harmattan winds. It seems they are collecting not just water from this magical dark pool, where the women stand now calf-deep, scooping water, and the crocodile rests only a few feet away, unmolesting. You can see the two bumps of his golden, marbled eyes above the water and the point of his snout. The crocodile rests as if he owns those women he surveys all day. As he watches, his eyes don't shift and are often closed. His snout is motionless—still, he seems confident and all-seeing, and when he slips back under and blows bubbles, I think the women are scooping something of him that he wants to give, a wild, unknown thing.

There once was a little girl, Kombaté told me, who put her head in the mouth of the crocodile and walked in. Down in his belly she found a fire and stools arranged around the fire. One stool fit her and she sat in it. Spirits and ancestors came to be warmed by the fire and to sing. Hearing their voices, she did not want to go back to the village—no! no! no! she wailed. Still, she did what they told her, what they sung to her. She pulled a rib from the crocodile's side until it broke, and when she climbed up his throat, she poked the roof of his mouth with the jagged point. As soon as he opened his mouth to complain, she jammed the bone so he could not close his mouth, and she walked back to the village. She grew up not telling anyone what the spirits and ancestors had sung to her. But her fields grew the greenest millet, she had the most beautiful children, her husband was enchanted with her and could not even look at another woman, and when she brought water back from the pond it glistened and brought happiness.

Now when I sit on the bank of the pond looking at the crocodile and his peerless eyes, I think about Kombaté's story and what the bush people are trying to tell me. Besides *nyobig*, there's *tiig* for tree like that baobab with bubbling bark, and there's *jual* for mountain whose rocks return at night no matter how many times the Europeans dynamite them (at least that's Kombaté's story). Pronouncing the Benga words makes me feel that the world must have such wild things in it. Occasionally, *nyobig* will yawn or gurgle or beg for another sardine from my can, and his mouth will open wide, and it will look inside as pink, dark and seemingly endless as I'd imagined. I will notice the sharp protruding scales that come out of his neck as he surfaces just a little. And at those times I feel an urge to wade over to him, just those several feet away, and put my head in his mouth and have a look around the unknown. Hah!

And this seems like it could be a totally normal feeling because the women are there fetching their water, babies tied to their backs, not even watching *nyobig* with his mouth askew. That dark, pink tunnel of unknown, is this where bush stories are born? Down there, might I hear some whisper from Mama, something of her that could not die?

Sometimes at night, when the crocodile's eyes are open and wide and you can see his two pupils fully rounded and shining in the dark like flashlight beams, *nyobig* pulls himself onto the shore. I see those twin-eyes lumber along and the shadow of a tail follows. I hear the clap-clap-clap of his jaws. Maybe he's grabbed somebody's chicken or a calabash of millet left out for him. I hurry up the cliff, past the baobab, past the curling-up smoke of Bibabé's fire, and back to camp, where Aunt and Uncle listen to the short-wave. The sky behind me looks like *nyobig* has climbed its bank, his jagged teeth aglow among the stars. Sometimes the I-don't-knows are mounting so high around me it seems like they'll swallow me up, like they did Mama. But then as I'm watching *nyobig* light up the sky, I realize he wants me to tell a story. A story is a mouth that can talk to another world, a wild world that turns God upside down. And what I don't know is a beginning.

But I'm only twelve and far from home. And the unknown lurks and ambushes, hidden, yet aware of my every move. The cliff rocks hover overhead. *Nyobig* floats in his shrinking pond. My toes sink into the soft, murky bottom that has no bottom. And I scoop up the little bubbles, the words, the stories about what I don't know.

FLIGHT 4590

Poem by Michael Hanner

Any fool can wait in an airport bar for someone
who isn't coming back. Christmas lights burn down.

Pick your blue; Dresden, royal, cerulean, indigo
or the color of the scarf of the virgin, her scarf.
They sat for an hour in the nave eating peppermints
filling their pockets with the sticky wrappers.

Saint Paul is just another ham sandwich to him,
but the light in Chartres Cathedral is the clear blue,
the same hue as the glass vase of daisies picked
for the flight attendant at *Cimetière de Passy*.
There is the moon and forgiveness and grace.

But no one is sure of much any more.

If there was a god, he would have worshiped Her.

Spend all his time praising Her divine etcetera.

He remembered this in the dark and wind
watching the lightning over Wenatchee.

He remembered Sara at twenty. Forgave himself.
again. there is the marrow and there is the bone.

The wind plays a dirge on the struts in bay bridge.

He's gone to Nice for the winter, hoping for kindness.

Later in the year, way past August, mosquitos,

the moon, Argyle. Ham on the bone,

But your eyes are still Christmas lights, sweetheart.
Waiting for *Le Poste* to come in its yellow van.
Her old passport tucked in a copy of Prévert

left in the bar on Herenstraat. Think of snow,

square knots. Brussels is always a square knot.

It sounded like a freight train going over, a witness said.
But we're back, heading for spring again, ready to be

slung 'round the sun again when light grows thin,

awaking in the night dreaming of the birch trees
on fire. *Welcome to the asylum.* She went down

in Gonesse, north of Paris—a punctured fuel tank
caused, someone said, by debris on the runway.

PROM NIGHT, 1961

Fiction by Jan Baross

Bakersfield, CA

My Willard was killed in a glider accident last week.

His father let him go up, and a rough wind brought him down. The glider broke apart, and so did Willard.

I went to the funeral, but I didn't cry. I wanted to. I thought I should. But tears make it real. It wasn't real for me. Not yet.

I slept a lot and kept thinking we would be dancing at the Prom like we planned. Well, sort of planned. Not that he'd asked me yet.

"So, the prom," he'd say. Sounding like he'd assumed.

And I'd wait for the real invite, not assuming.

That was as far as we got in our last conversation.

I pictured Willard in his light blue tux. If I believed in crap like heaven, then, sure, we'd be in touch again. He'd be scuffing up the heaven with his big shoes, trying to lead me on some golden dance floor, other dead couples dancing to songs they remembered. "Rock around the Clock." That was our song.

Keeping that story in my head, that's what kept me together. It wasn't really prom night without Willard. But Mother said I had to go.

"You don't want to look back in twenty years," said Mother, "and wished you'd gone to your prom. Remember, everything you do enriches your life. Someday you'll thank me."

I wondered when that "someday" would come, when I'd be grateful for the million things she made me do that I didn't want to do. I always felt like I was fighting just to breathe my own air.

Mother railroaded on ahead and set me up for the Prom with her bridge friend's son. Hiram. Who names their kid Hiram?

Mother parked us in front of Dory Derry Berry's Shop for Women.

Several mothers and daughters were sitting in Dory's waiting room. Graduation was when places like this raked it in.

"Glad I made an appointment." Mother whisked us through to front of the line. I got measured, fitted and finalized.

All I could think was, what a waste of time and money. We were going to wear these gorgeous formals once. Just once on a hot Bakersfield night. Guys with their sweaty hands all over our taffeta. And then what? Bag it and save it for our daughters who would one day say, "But it's so old-fashioned!"

Mother looked up from her best seller and smiled at my red dress. The fit would've shown cleavage if I had any. So, all in all, a good package, if you weren't a tit man.

And Willard, he would have crawled into that light blue tux that probably smelled like moth balls. He'd take one gawky look at the results of all Mother's efforts with one question on his mind. Like, how can I touch what's under that dress?

Goddamit, Willard! Can you see me down here? You promised to take me into space!

The doorbell rang. My first blind date. Hiram stood there like he was in front of a firing squad. Reed-tall, severe haircut, smart, skittery eyes behind thick glasses. Award winner on the debate team. He shackled my wrist with a gardenia corsage and led me to the car.

I didn't let him hold my hand walking toward the cafeteria. I was embarrassed to be seen with him. For one thing, you don't want to look too smart at Bakersfield High, and he did.

Inside the cafeteria, it was a swamp. Wilted crepe from condensed kid sweat. Music amped too loud. The band was totally off beat. I heard the drummer had broken his arm at the annual James Dean drag race. A lot of the kids were standing around drinking punch, some danced, others signing the carboard mascot. A few nicer kids came up and said, "Sorry to hear about Willard."

"Thanks for reminding me," I said.

I slumped into one of the foldout chairs. Hiram brought over two plastic cups of red punch. He set one in front of me and sat down. I saw red on his cuff. I didn't thank him.

"You should be nicer to me," Hiram shouted over the band. "I spent three bucks on your corsage."

I took the gardenia off my wrist and threw it at him.

"Get a refund," I shouted.

Jesus! Take it out on Hiram because he's not Willard. You are a shit!

"Okay, Hollis," I shouted, "I'm sorry."

"Hiram," he shouted.

He was just a nice guy who'd make someone a nice husband if that's all you wanted. He had no idea what to do with someone like me. I should have come to the prom alone, but no one does that.

"Why'd you want to come to the prom with me?" he shouted.

"I didn't want to come at all," I shouted. "My mother set this up. Because my boyfriend got killed."

"Oh. Ok. Sorry for that. But I seem to annoy you," he shouted. "Maybe I should leave you alone?"

"Would you? Please," I shouted back. "Catch me in an hour. You can take me home."

Hiram put his punch cup down, got up and walked away from me. What a relief.

But to his credit, he had responded to my pissiness like a grown up. Left me to rant alone. I respected that. But I really did just want to go home.

Hiram beelined to Marlee, a thin wallflower-type genius with glasses. Never mind who her date was. She and Hiram fit together like the last two pieces of a puzzle. He'd probably marry her, and they'd have kids, and he'd work his way up in the new aerospace industry and die bald. Maybe they'd have true love. Something I figured would never find me. Willard dead. I couldn't cry. Who'd marry someone like that?

Mary Ellen was dancing with Rolly. I was jealous. Now I wanted a queer boyfriend too. Rolly's tan glowed and his black hair rested over his collar, a real dangerous look. He was getting ready to go out in the world and make his debut. "Broadway, here I come!" And Mary Ellen, with her red hair. She wore it free and wavy. She was ready to leave her crazy family behind and waft out of here onto the stage of any summer stock that would have her. There was something wild and full of neon promise about those two tonight.

I did what I always do when I get stuck. I whipped out my pencil, and I drew anything that didn't move too fast. The butcher paper tablecloth was a blessing.

"Get yourself a hobby that doesn't rely on other people," Mother always said.

Out of the corner of my eye, I sketched Darrel the quarterback with his team buddies chugging from a not-very-hidden pint. Lucky for them the chaperones were flirting among themselves. Darrel got caught once with vodka in his snow cone and was almost expelled.

Mary Ellen and Rolly saw I was alone and sat down next to me. A spread of green taffeta formal around Mary Ellen's ankles. Rolly looked like a Fred Astair chorus boy in his tight tux.

"Lemme see what you did," Mary Ellen shouted over the band noise.

I tore off my sketch and handed it to her. She was my biggest fan because I always made people look uglier than they were.

"Memories," she said, and stuffed the sketch in her purse.

"Where's your date," she shouted and drank my punch.

I nodded at Hiram dancing eyeglasses to eyeglasses with his future bride.

"Prince Dreary," I shouted.

Mary Ellen nodded, took off her heels and gave her toes a pull.

"The biggest launch party of our lives," shouted Rolly, "Look at us!"

"Oh, fuck this shit" shouted Mary Ellen, "I can't hear a thing!"

She shoved her feet back in the heels. The three of us pushed through the cafeteria's double doors. Ah Lord, that hot breeze sucked my sweat dry. A full moon lit up the quad. We sank onto the cement benches. A couple was making out and scooted away. One woozy guy passed us a pint. I took a big slug and felt good.

"Where is it written," said Rolly, "that graduates can't celebrate their liberation at the site of their own choosing?"

That's just what I was thinking, only not as elegantly stated.

"Let's take a drive!" said Mary Ellen.

We got up and straightened out our damp creases.

"I should say goodbye to Hiram," I said.

"Hiram's found the love of his creepy life," said Mary Ellen. "Let's boogie."

Ten minutes later we were driving along Chester Avenue crammed in the front seat of Rolly's father's Pontiac. Rolly pulled out his own pint from under the seat. We shared it to empty. We were flying high.

"Where you guys wanna go?" said Rolly, pulling up to a red light and gunning his motor.

That question always brought out the best in me.

"Venice," I said. When they laughed, I said. "Venice Beach."

Mary Ellen got it right away, clapped me on the knee. "You're thinking we find the Beats?"

"I'm thinking The Gas House!" I said. It was Beatnik central. We'd read about King of The Beats, Big Daddy Nord, who owned the Gas House Cafe. I'd had a big itch for a while to rub myself raw against their scruffy lives.

"Ladies, you pay for the gas," said Rolly.

A whole evening ahead of us!

"Fuck all!" shouted Rolly and tossed the empty pint out the window. It shattered against a metal mailbox. We looked around to see if any cops saw that. Then we laughed, a nervous laugh. I mean, we weren't thugs.

We didn't know where Venice Beach was. But we knew the way out of town.

The Pontiac roared along Highway 99 with the windows wide open.

"Three little maids from school are we, filled to the brim with girlish glee." We sang all the Gilbert and Sullivan songs we knew. That got us up the ridge route, through the dusty Tehachapis, all the way to the City of Angels.

Rolly pulled over to a lit-up café. We needed coffee bad. Sitting at the counter, my head started clearing. I looked at the clock on the wall. It had taken us two hours to get here. It was nine. We weren't even at Venice Beach. Two hours and some to get back. Mother said to be home no later than one. That meant we had to leave Venice before eleven.

"We've got forty-five minutes to find the Beats," I said.

"No problem," said Mary Ellen and asked the old waitress where Venice Beach was. She didn't know. She lived above the café with her husband and had never been very far down the road.

"Look at you kids." she said. She shoved the sugar and cream at us. "My prom night was the best night of my life. Then I got married."

There was a truck driver sitting on one of the stools. He said his name was Burly and he offered to draw us a map to Venice Beach.

"You kids stop at the Gas House," said the truck driver. "They got great cinnamon rolls. Lemme show you."

We jumped in the car. Time was running out. Even with the map, Rolly got us lost.

Finally, a sign: To Venice Beach. We turned south from Market to Ocean Front Walk. Rolly swung the car into a small side street and parked.

We jumped out and ran a block to the boardwalk that paralleled a wide sandy beach and a moonlit sea. From the moment we stepped into the flow of strangers we got swept up into a crazy costumed swirl of painted dancers, half naked humanity, song singers on skates, clowns balanced on stilts juggling stars. We passed shops spray-painted wild.

I felt so tingling alive. This circus was pure oxygen. The three of us were kind of freaky. But here's where freakdom were born.

Time was ticking. "We gotta find the Gas House quick," I said.

Mary Ellen jabbed me. "There it is!"

We ran for the two-story building with four huge painted pillars. Slumped Beatniks dressed in black under the Gas House sign with cigarette butts shinning orange. Some herded around the door. Heart-thudding music from inside. "The West Coast Wailing Wall of the Dispossessed." That's what a newspaper called it.

A cute guy in a black turtleneck blew a jet of acrid-smelling smoke at me and handed over his wrinkled cigarette. I didn't know what to make of such an unsanitary gesture. Beats smoked marijuana. No one ever said it involved sharesies.

Mary Ellen grabbed the cig from me and inhaled deep just like the Beats around us. They were talking through constricted throats, holding in the smoke.

Rolly inhaled and got a little dreamy eyed. He passed it back to me, so I tried a tepid inhale and choked. That got some laughs. Not the kind I liked.

We hurried to the door, paid the small entrance fee and got a dark green GH stamped on our hand. Inside it was hot. The music was a chest hammer. A girl on stage moved like an angry toy and belted out her song with a gravel voice.

"Janis!' the crowd screamed.

Mary Ellen pointed to Big Daddy Nord. We'd seen his picture in the newspaper: six feet eight, 400 pounds, dark beard, a captain's hat. I wished I'd brought my poetry notebook to show him. He was focused on something over my head.

I turned and saw this tall skinny guy in a red sweater.

Holly shit. It was Mort Sahl, the funniest comedian on the planet. I had all this guy's albums. I knew his routines by heart. Nord seemed really glad to see him. Mort waved at me.

"Hey, Crimson Sally, right?" said Mort.

I was anybody he wanted me to be. "Yeah. Right, Purple Onion," I said. "Good to see you Mort."

An exhalation of larky girls surrounded him with their autograph books and shoved me right out of his limelight.

So, this where life had been keeping itself! In a grand old coffee house by the sea. I was inhaling memory, even as it happened. Daddy Nord's arsenal of abandon. I kissed my green inked hand. My passport. Welcome to the Gas House. I was home.

I dragged on another reefer offered, deeper this time. It hit me like a soft cloud, a Gas House doped up breeze. Dancing with bodies. My brain bathed in the staccato light show, Janis, her vortex voice. I was a cloud climber!

Where were Rolly and Mary Ellen? It didn't matter. I danced and snaked and jerked like Janis down among the friendly, bellowy bandstand herd. And then I saw him.

At the edge of the crowd. A light blue tux. Willard?

I swam toward him, through the thick waves of weed-smelling bodies. I pushed ahead, but like the sea the crowd kept closing back in.

I could see his light blue color on the move.

"Wait!" I shoved closer, closer. Until there was nowhere to go. Right in front of me, on the wall. A Day-Glo poster. Light blue. A rock star.

But I had seen Willard's face. I looked around, my head rolling. "Willard!" His name kept disappearing in the drum strokes.

Mary Ellen grabbed me. "What's the problem? You look freaky."

"Willard," I yelled.

Rolly put his arm around me. "Hey. Let's find you a quiet place."

We ended up in a moldy office. Rolly shut the door but the sound came through.

I was crying. Crying like I hadn't let myself. Even to breathe. Not stopping. God, how could a friend just go? Just go like that?

Mary Ellen held me. "Now. Now. Remember," she said. "You weren't really in love with him."

"Shut up, Mar," said Rolly. "Cry it all out, kiddo. He was a great guy. I miss him too."

"You hardly knew him," said Mary Ellen

"I knew him enough," said Rolly. "Will you shut the fuck up!"

"Leave me alone!" I sobbed.

I was on the floor, crumbling from the hard cry. Mary Ellen reached to help me back up. I saw her gold graduation watch, like a loud wake-up bell. I snorted back my tears.

"Christ! What time is it?"

Mary Ellen held out the watch for me to see.

"It's one AM," she said. "Wow, the next day. We graduated yesterday."

"Holy shit. I'm supposed to be home by one!" I said.

A huge man opened the door, filled the frame and nearly shut out the light show behind him. No mistake who that was.

"Mr. Nord," said Mary Ellen, "May we use this phone? We got a parental crisis here."

"Sure," he said. "Happens all the time."

He grabbed a plastic bag from his desk drawer.

"If it's long distance, make it short." he said.

Mary Ellen threw Big Daddy Nord a kiss. He grinned and ambled out.

I picked up the phone, heard the dial tone and put it down.

"What the hell am I going to say?" I said.

"The old shuffle game," Mary Ellen said, "Tell them you're partying at my house and you'll be home in the morning. I'll tell mine I'm at yours. Rolly, his parents don't worry. Hang up fast before they ask any questions."

An obvious veteran in these matters. But I was shaking.

I picked up the phone again. The mouthpiece looked big enough to swallow me.

Mary Ellen dialed for me.

"Is that you?" It was Daddy's voice. Not his kind sweet patient voice. What I heard was exhaustion.

"Your Mother's pretty upset," he said.

We both knew that was an understatement. What had Mother's panic done to him? What would she do to me?

"It's just 1:00," I said.

"No," he said, "It's 1:30."

Shit! Typical! Her new watch, late as she was.

"I'm sorry, Daddy," I said. "Mary Ellen's watch was off. But don't worry. We're safe and still partying at Mary Ellen's. The girl's impromptu slumber party. I'll be home in the morning. You only graduate once. Right? I gotta go."

Bang. I hung up.

Oh shit. I'd never lied to Daddy. Mother, sure, but Daddy.

"Think he bought it?" said Mary Ellen.

"How the hell do I know?" I said.

Of course, he didn't buy it. I'd never spoken to him like that before.

I was paying a high price for my big night. So were the folks.

I pictured Mother pacing in panic, looking at her watch, the two of them wearing a groove in the beige wall to wall. It wasn't hard to project my return. Daddy at the curb, me getting out of the car with sun coming up.

"You're home," he'd say, as if he'd been holding his breath. Relief. I could count on his relief. He would hug his short sleeve warmth into me. I would smell his long sour night of fear. What it took to keep Mother sane.

I was already ashamed of what I'd done it to him. He had always treated me like an adult, linked his arm in mine when we walked together. He would do that, link arms and we would face the house where Mother lived, waited, stewed. Seeing my sorry face would boil her right over the top. I never wanted to go home.

"I have to go home," I said.

Rolly swayed and handed me his keys. Clearly, I was the designated driver.

Outside the Gas House, a night sea smelled so fresh. The two of them climbed into the back seat of the car, curled up together, happy, wasted, and fell asleep.

Windows wide open, I drove us slowly in the opposite direction of the Beat's siren song. Feeling my way from memory, it seemed like forever. The highway night got grayer, bluer, brighter then opened up finally to day.

Once we reached the tan foothills of the Tehachapis, I drove a little faster toward home. The terror was subsiding. A calmness seemed to come out of nowhere like another kind of high in the mountain air. Descending back into the dry San Joaquin Valley, I had the vague sensation of a temporary sentence.

I owed Mother and Daddy a grand apology. It wouldn't come out of fear. Prom night. The initiation was over. Something inevitable had been set in motion.

My journey, our journeys, had finally, finally begun.

PART II

LOVERS

Poem by Mallory Kellum

One of her lovers was a robin, the other a glove.
One was a pebble, the other a pond.

She would wear her red coat out,
strolling through autumn's night song.

One of her lovers was the shadow of champagne,
the other the freckled sky stealing the moon's throne.

One was an orange slice, the other a sorrowful sun;
both joined by their distant smile.

She was the lace tucked away just in case.

IN BETWEEN

Poem by Susan Donnelly

It is not the first
nor the last that matter;
it is the glorious, terrifying,
and often mundane moments
in between that toll
the major cords.
Deep breaths, full hearts,
and the juicy rare meat
at the center of the roast;
the gray-haired fourth-grade teacher
who convinced us
we were smart and beautiful,
and the high-heeled blonde
fifth-grade one who proved
we were not.
The ruby-throated hummingbird
hovering outside the window in February;
our slaughtered sisters
and buried brothers
who leave us forever wondering
why we have been spared.
Phone numbers memorized
without really trying, the friends
forgotten, lost in the race.
Rains that never arrived
to water our shriveled seeds,
and the ones that raised river levels,
leaving mold on our hopes.
Sins we confessed

and ones we dared
not whisper even to ourselves.
Loyal dogs cuddled on cold nights
and the soulful-eyed-shelter-ones
who barked too much;
a brittle bite of dark chocolate,
endless hours of solitaire,
a warm ray of springshine,
and the redeeming smiles
of total strangers
and those we have known
forever.

LOUIS

Nonfiction by Hayley McCoy

My ghosts visit me sometimes. They come back to me, like wisps, edges of fog, reminding me of my broken places that have been patched over time.

I draw out this memory, like a blanket from a long-forgotten chest. Holding it soft to my face, I am transported instantly, in that magical way that scent can transcend the present, to deposit me, ready or not, into the past.

My sociology professor sits across from me. His name is Louis Hardeman. He is tall, black, and young, but I am younger and barely notice. We sit at a table in the cafeteria, beside the giant wall of windows. I want to discuss Sociology 101. But he doesn't give me the chance.

"Does your mother know you're wearing *flip-flops*...in November?" "Flip-flops" spits out of his mouth: challenging, incredulous, but something a little like awe, too.

I take it as a compliment. My rubber slippers are slightly too small for my feet, just how I have always worn them, and bright orange. We call them slippers in the Philippines, not flip-flops.

But I don't tell him this. Instead, I press my lips into a polite smile. He leans slightly forward, his towering frame perching on the hard chair; his imposing constitution matches his larger-than-life personality. In stark contrast to the day's bleakness, his luminous eyes radiate intensity. Too piercing, too acute. I divert my focus to the windows overlooking the bare trees that not so long ago were covered in beautiful New England red, yellow, and orange foliage. Now the stemmy branches stretch across the gray backdrop of the sky.

My gaze travels down to the table in front of me, down to my hands, resting so patiently on my pile of lecture notes in front of me. I stay mute, resolute. I expect him to ignore his own inquiry—as I am—and move on to the paramount subject at hand: his course.

But he doesn't. He waits, silently.

He is staring at me, and his face simulates the look he holds in his lectures when emphasizing a crucial point: half smiling, eyebrows raised, head tilted, almost imperceptibly, to one side.

I feel he can see through me, and he knows that I don't belong here. My fingers start rifling through the yellow sticky notes butting from the edges of my papers. He bends sideways and peers under the table. His eyes flicker back to mine, as if to prove that he has seen my ridiculous flip-flops; that denial is useless.

The concern in his countenance unsettles me. He seems almost worried about my lack of warm shoes, as if that were more significant than his lectures. As if my well-being should be considered. As if I might be important.

Unused to this sentiment, I deflect, laughing, hiding my embarrassment.

His large hands splay flat on the table, he leans in further. All signs of mirth gone, "Hayley Stevenson," the timbre of his voice serious, as he carves out my full name, as if I am being particularly problematic. His voice unyielding. "I asked you a question. Does your mother know about this?" He gestures with one hand in the general direction of my feet.

It dawns on me then, he is determined to persevere. The truth is, my feet are freezing, but it didn't even occur to me to not wear my slippers. In the Philippines, we wear slippers all year.

Flustered, I mumble the lame response, "My mum is far away."

His gaze still fixated on me, I straighten the pile of papers in front of me, nudging them just a bit closer to him, as a reminder. And, mercifully, he moves on to the matters of his class.

When my last yellow sticky note has been addressed, I promptly commence my escape, heading for the door, for fresh air, and the sweet attraction of oblivion. I exhale in relief.

"Hayley!" His booming voice reverberates against my back. Startled, I turn. His arm extended, he is pointing at me and attempting, unsuccessfully, to suppress a smile. "I don't want to see you wearing flip-flops anymore—it's *November!*"

I hesitate, debating how much to let him care. In that instant, his arm drops, his posture softens, eyes seeking mine, as if a tenderness has washed over him. Eager to avoid any more fuss, I raise my hand slightly, to show that I heard, and nodding madly—in what I hope will be interpreted as compliance—I scurry away. Hot with the self-consciousness of unexpected compassion and wary of his regard, I never request another meeting with him.

I love my slippers, and I refuse to give them up. I continue to wear them all through fall semester, even to Sociology 101. The small classroom is cramped, packed full of students shimmying sideways down the narrow aisles of one-armed desks, as if attempting to get to the window seat on an airplane. I sit toward the far end of the classroom, far enough from possible scrutiny, but near enough to melt in with the others.

Dr. Louis Hardeman begins his lecture with urgency, pacing back and forth in front of the classroom. His arms go up and down in sync to the beat of his words. He dances us into answering his questions: *it's privilege, racism, distribution of wealth.* Then, like a baseball catcher, he crouches down to eye level with us: *It's all your point of view.*

He is magnetic. I can't look away.

He tries to divide up the class in teams: blue-and-green-eyed people versus brown-eyed people—"So arbitrary!" he exclaims. But there are too many of us in the overcrowded classroom, and we can't move about to rearrange into our arbitrary teams, so we stay where we are. But everyone says they *get it*. Still, I feel I'm at a disadvantage being on the opposite team from him.

Scanning the room, head tilted, eyebrows raised, he talks about the things that are *revolutionary*. I don't really understand, but when he looks my way, I tuck my toes safely under my desk and nod along with the others.

Sociology 101 is the only class Dr. Hardeman teaches for nonmajors, so I never have another class with him again. But later that winter, it got cold—so frigid—it hurt to breathe. Long, slender icicles reaching down from high, steep roofs; earth covered in crunchy, crystal snow, sharp enough to make cuts in the sides of my feet. My thoughts flicker back to him peeking at my flip-flops, and I learn about winter boots and trudge through the next three years, long enough to graduate.

That encounter was buried under the years of life that pile like wet leaves in the forest. It wasn't until fifteen years later that I even thought of him again, when someone told me that he had passed away, taking his own life. I was shocked. Details were smudged under the general guise that "things had been tough" for him. Things were *tough* for this man? This person whose radiance blazed bright against the desolate northern winter? This professor who seemed to embody more ardor and zeal than anyone else I had come across in those long years of study?

Disconcerted, and staring in the face of my unforeseen heartache, I went to the public library and looked up anything I could find about Dr. Louis Hardeman on the Internet. I discovered he had grown up in Boston, he had never married, had no children. I read about his accomplishments and his education, graduating with honors, and how, right out of graduate school, he became a professor of sociology.

I sit back, letting the screen go black. I close my eyes, remembering.

He appears as a ghost before me. Like the forgotten blanket that holds a place in its essence, I am transported. I find I am again sitting at the table, with numbed toes shoved into orange rubber slippers, face flushed, trying to talk about social structures of America, and trying not to talk about my mum, and desperately trying to act like I belong there.

He sits before me, questioning, "Does your mother know you're wearing flip-flops in November?"

His bright eyes are intense, but this time, I don't look away.

I dare to do it differently.

I tell him about my family in the Philippines and how we huddle under a blanket when it gets "cold," the same weather during which people here would be wearing tank tops and cheering about "summer." No, my mum wouldn't care about flip-flops and wouldn't know about being "cold."

But then again, neither do I. I'm not from here.

He responds with his own truth. He tells me how arduous it was for him in academia, and how hard he had fought to make it as a professor in the stuffy, mostly white New England college. That he never felt like he fit in, but despite it all, he cared about his students, and he would keep fighting.

He stands to leave, but I'm not ready to let him ghost away, and I follow him to his class. He begins lecturing, pacing, gesturing—familiarity rushes over me instantly. There is fire in his eyes, vehemence in his voice, as he tries to make us truly comprehend the social inequity, the racism, the disparity of wealth in America. He pauses when he makes his most critical point, half smiling, eyebrows raised, head tilted, just barely. His countenance pleading and demanding, asking: *Do you get it?*

New to the country, I had found the cultural undertones difficult to grasp. I hadn't realized that the fiery lectures on racism and prejudice that burst out of him are his own story.

Now I see his need for us to understand had been personal.

As I turn to leave, his loud yell rumbles out from behind me, "Hayley!"

In the foggy evening, he stands straight, his eyes shining, his arm reaching out to me, pointing. He's smiling and scolding, "Put away those flip-flops—it's *November*!" And I...I let him care.

I raise my hand in a salute, "Yessir," not even trying to hide my own smile. He knows something that I don't: that no one who lives here could possibly wear flip-flops all year.

I would never belong there, but that was beside the point. He knew something else I had yet to understand. That reaching out in kindness was an act of compassion that could save someone. That choosing to connect was *revolutionary*.

I wish I could tell him it meant something that he had cared. That his act of kindness became a patch in my brokenness; far from exposing me, it held me together. That in noticing the insignificant, he had whispered, *you matter.*

And yet, while I had been unaware of his influence, it had always been there.

For I have an eight-year-old son, and I named him Louis.

WHAT HISTORY MAKES OF US

Poem by Marie Hartung

An old Tibetan saying says
to set fire to the wood,
you need the help of the wind.

At the mouth of the river
the unzipped sky is shamefully manhandled
The ocean tilts on its broken axis.

It wasn't just me with the matches.
Just after midday, sun and language
burn a fat fist through dawn

and the citron of shadows
drape like a cloak of death
floating a bouquet of black tulips

on the endless shutter of waves.
Where two things meet,
we welcome the flap and panic

of moss-fruited water, the salt-stained
lips of possible loss. In your lips
you purse the matchbox tight.

I can't tell from here if it's empty,
or full, regulator of mind and mouth.
The smoldering upriver desiccates

sand under our knees. You drop
the matchbook and a boney wave
grabs it, renders it useless.
The pressed sky looks away, ashamed.
I burn the wood and drain the river.
Who knows what clouds swallowed you?

When the wind finally sashays along
it blows my hair to smithereens.
Nothing here changes—unoriginal dimming

casts toward what I have not seen

and won't still. In the blended current
of forgetting, the memory is a trespass.

New alders sprout like stars
along the banks in the mute dark.
The regrettable sky chokes tears, knowing what's coming.

SUBTLE ARTS

Nonfiction by Billie Hudson

I.
Chad, the associate dean, had that book *The Subtle Art of Not Giving a F*ck* sitting on his desk. It struck me as a poor choice for the dean in charge of equity, even if he was about to retire.

II.
My father used to sit me down in high school to explain that I was a smart girl, and that boys find smart girls intimidating.

III.
Chad, the associate dean, was responsible for following procedure and ensuring that others did too. But he was also practicing the art of not giving a fuck. Although he had not shown up for the interview, he responded confidently to yet another woman complaining to him about sexism, "No sexism was visible to me."
   Exactly.

IV.
As the smart girl on the shortlist, I do not have this luxury: *not* giving a fuck is not a fucking option for me. Instead, I puzzle for months over the right thing to wear on the interview, not to mention what I will say. I decide on a playful pinstripe skirt with vertical stripes in the middle and horizontal stripes on the hem and waistband. I have it taken in because the stress has me losing weight.
   In the weeks leading up to the interview, I work out on my preferred elliptical machine at the back of the Y, training for the interview as if preparing for a fight. I watch the minutes tick, climbing imaginary stairs to "Girl on Fire." Ten minutes into my workout, I think, *By now, I will*

have finished the introduction. Twenty minutes in, *Now I'll be half-way through my talk.* I prepare for anything as I picture myself standing in a swanky room, in a swanky building, at a swanky university.

V.

I have to care because the stakes are high. I've been commuting seventy miles away from my family on the most heavily trafficked truck route in the area for years, toting my breast pump on the morning Greyhound. I often miss breakfast, but never leave without doing my daughter's hair. She's up early every time, anticipating this intimate ritual on our green couch. I learned early that to miss it was an undoing for her and for me, destabilizing our precious ecosystem. During her eight years of life, my eight years of commuting, I forgot only one time, embarking too hastily on a frazzled drive to work. When I realized the error, I turned around and returned home. Later, as my relationship disintegrates and the tension at home mounts, she asks me to just keep brushing her hair. We cling to this extended ritual, the two of us, to keep the chaos at bay.

At the other end of my day, after I survive the rush hour return home, my son reclaims me from the outside world, pulling me back into our shared life to nurse his way into a delicious slumber. This means that I must always return before his bedtime. Whereas my daughter was done with nursing at the age of one, my son stretches this ritual well past two, worshiping the intimacy that ensures my timely return home.

One time, I receive a call from state police shortly after I arrive. They ask why I failed to pay for gas at the highway gas station on my way home. Flustered, I explain that I stop there routinely and would never intentionally dodge my bill. The officer takes pity as my frustrated two year-old demands I return to his bedtime rituals.

VI.

The first time that I spent a night away from my first-born was when she was about to turn one. I took two flights to give a talk in Georgia, and my breast pump broke on the way there. I gave my talk that evening in agony, performing before a crowded auditorium, fearful my breasts would erupt. I was the only woman on the panel. As my silver-haired panelists remain seated, serene on the stage, I rise to perform, projecting, and gesticulating as I make eye contact, all the while hoping the milk does not breach the final levy to discolor the bright red stripes sewn across the front of my black fitted dress. Afterward, the other panelists congratulate me on my vivacious offering.

The next morning, another professor I have just met mercifully lends me her breast pump. I enter a pumping room after asking three library employees how to access the key. That key unlocks a secret world, a small room barren but for a notepad pulsating with encouragement and frustration in notes passed among working women as they pump. That afternoon, when I deposit my breastmilk on the scanner, a crowd of male TSA employees surround the bag of yellowish liquid, asking one another what it is.

VII.

Nose pressed up against the glass of another life, I find my frustration turns to yearning for the peace of proximity. There is the small matter of work, eight years in a job so far from two small children means despair for the opening two miles from home. It's not the ivy-covered Gothic buildings or the number of books in the library I obsess over, but the number of ways to commute safely home, liberated from the highway normally traveled. One could walk and, in fact, I discuss this with Dawn, the Fitbit-obsessed administrative assistant: "How many steps to the East Side?" One could bike, braving city drivers on edge. Or hop a tram. This last one is my favorite: home in twenty minutes. Put in a full day at work and still take the kids for gelato after school, long enough before dinnertime. One could also run. Change in the office, leave a bag there, savor the freedom all the way home.

VIII.

Academic interviews are grueling endurance tests. They span two long days that include public presentations, interviews with committees, meals, drinks, and countless private interviews with faculty, students, and university administration.

When the first interview day begins, I roam the halls between meetings, peering into slim rectangular windows of faculty offices, picturing myself in them. Books stand at attention, neatly aligned on white shelves perched on white walls, below which sit shiny new white tables, round and rectangular, and meticulous white couches. I search for signs of life and the familiar chaos of the professor's office, but nary a pencil or stray paper finds its way to linger on cleared surfaces. They remain sewn up, uninhabited, little circulation of air or ideas. Doors are locked before and behind me as I move through each meeting. It's as if this building needs a little mess, a little me.

Dawn follows behind me, locking her office, the seminar room, the bathroom. I imagine uptight memos issued by the school's director, eschewing the messy desk's fertile mind, opting instead for the optics of anal retention. Or had this all been accomplished by racialized workers, brought in under the cover of night to bring white spaces under tight control? I imagine Brendan, the school's director, drafting a memo late one night after glimpsing a particularly egregious office out of order. *Offices shall be inspected routinely for stray papers, noncompliant occupants evicted.*

IX.

Gay people can be really mean to one another. During our private meeting, Brendan pisses on the ground around him. After mentioning that his research is starting to get into my territory, he explains that the senior position for which I am interviewing will complement his own. He congratulates me for the $198,000 grant I was just awarded. I tell him about my proposal to create a new lab, asking if there would be space at the school. He ponders this and replies that he can think of someone he'd like very much to evict to make space available. When I explain that the next deadline for the submission is soon, he suggests that he put his own name on my proposal in order to submit it, as a favor.

As I grin in response to convey gratitude, red ticker tape runs slowly across the back of my eyes: N O F U C K I N G W A Y.

He asks how many children I have, and their ages. "Don't worry," I want to say, "I'm done, and my reproductive cycle is too."

But that would be a lie, and I answer truthfully because I'm the job candidate performing like a clever monkey in my playful pinstripe skirt.

X.

In my public lecture, I rattle off the books I've written, proud of their covers, the awards they've garnered, even the font of their titles, proud of the fact that they exist at all, the weight of them containing so much life unwritten in the text.

To a sea of white faces, I speak about displacement and immigration in a global city. When I finish, white men speak uninterrupted for fifty minutes. They attempt to berate, challenge, and dismiss. The women in the room look on, mortified in their silence. A younger scholar later tells me he texted a friend while enraged during the Q & A, "Only POC in room."

The former director of the school wanders in late, whispers in the ear of the current director during the talk, then leaves before the Q & A begins.

It's one of those Q & As with questions-that-aren't-questions. You know the kind. I carry myself carefully, positioning my body to demonstrate attentiveness and authority in equal doses. A career's worth of experiences prepared me for this.

XI.

How did I navigate those whitewashed control zones? I had my heaviest period on the day of the interview. Between performances, moving from one locked interior to another, I frequent an infrequently used room: the ladies near administration. I close the door and breathe, release a gush of blood, flush, zip up my corporate-sexy, wash, apply lipstick, return to the fray. A couple of times, I stop to write in my orange notebook in the only place I am not under surveillance. Sometimes job candidates will be given a floating office, time off between engagements to collect their thoughts. Mine is the women's bathroom. It seems important to bleed in private, given how few people in this building bleed at all.

XII.
After months of preparation, I take flight during the interview, propelled to new heights. It's as if this suffocating old building has been waiting for someone to breathe life into it. Others witness this technicolor expedition, weaving me into the fabric of their hopes too. I find myself atop of the city's towers, alighting in its phallic core. Potential female students and colleagues approach me hungrily to share how alienated they have felt in this building amid its current tenants, how they too yearn for something different. They embrace me, bathe me in enthusiasm, ask to meet the next day. They watch me handle the men, imagine me deft, their gay messiah—the lesbian femme fatale who can take on (name that asshole) in any setting and win. They text, "Nailed it. Loved it. Please come. We need you."

XIII.
Right after being told that the search committee favors my candidacy and will meet the following week to continue deliberations, I receive the following email: "The committee has decided not to hire this year."

The intricate dance between desire and rage continues: the things we hoped for that were never ours to lose. After this particular dream of proximity is squashed, female colleagues will fight for months. They phone the president, file grievances, and march into the dean of equity to complain about sexism—the very one practicing you know which art.

I picture myself having bled after all on the modern white furniture. Anger takes up residence in my messy body, uncontainable. For six straight nights I take Ambien to sleep, and then I go cold turkey off the pills. For months I exercise and write, exercise and write, to avoid the alternative: drink, sleeping pill, drink, sleeping pill.

Even my daughter—at eight—is angry when she finds out that no one got the job. "What was the point of all of that work?" As I try to hide my rage, I realize that she has already begun to develop her own.

XIV.

Another queer, feminist academic friend sends me a lengthy expose in a national newspaper about women scientists excluded for decades from the riches of a gene lab in California. The story's repetition exhausts me. I can't get through the whole thing, but I try out of respect for everything they went through.

XV.

Eleven straight white men and one queer brown woman—my friend Jude—drink Scotch late one night toward the end of a conference in a lavish hotel room high in the sky downtown. Their conversation turns to the recent job search where they interviewed three men and one woman. David looms over Jude as he explains a little too loudly how unimpressed he had been by the candidates. Then, afterward, he'd heard that people were so angry about the outcome that they were calling the president's office about sexism. "She's a sore loser," he barks, "using her power to influence the outcome."

"He's just mad that your publication record is so much bigger than his," Jude half-jokes as she shares this story.

XVI.

Eventually I learn that there were changes to university hiring policy as a result of errors in this interview. The associate dean is now required to actually attend interviews, pretending that he gives a fuck. Committee members must sign attendance sheets and attest to gender balance. There are ramifications for the people involved—for their own aspirations and the political fall-out they will contend with. None of this commutes my commute.

XVII.

Years ago, there was a persistent man I refused to date. He went around trashing me as a "lesbian convert," without sharing the part about his harassment. One of his closest friends was the head administrator receiving the complaints. In darker moments, I wonder if I had allowed Frank to actually fuck me as he'd hoped, then would his pals at this school not be fucking me now?

Unable to speak back to anyone without damaging my own career, messages come to me from the women who filed complaints. But if women aren't allowed to be smart, they sure as hell aren't allowed to be angry. Better to practice more subtle arts.

FRIDAY MOUTH

Poem by Jen Currin

Vocally, from my belly.
From my antlers hang jewels, necklaces
belonging to my grandmothers
and a very large pine cone
my aunt carried around in a cedar box
on her walks.
Witness: here for the ancestors
who call me on creaking phones
in the deep black vitality of night—
I'm sleeping.
Conversations twinkle
the next day, little dusts—
I must make notes.
Reminded again to love
the student who wrote problematic—
What she's trying to work out—
Difficult—lungs buck a little
as I bike up the rainy hill
& think of the great American poet in Paris,
compose a letter:
How are you & I heard
another one of your husbands died?
But now's the time to get up
& take some tincture.
Someone I love is leaving
for work & I watch
her slip an earring
into a lobe, lipstick her Friday mouth.
Later I will meet her—

keep my soul in a backpack
so it may be weighed
when I arrive.

OCEAN BIRD WOMAN

Nonfiction by Ciel Downing

I am in the winter of my years now. An elder who was once honored with a name that has come to define not just me, so much as my world and my connection to it. Most of my first forty years were spent walking the Red Path—subscribing to the Native Ways of moving through the world. At times, I lapse and only later recognize it when I note that I am out of balance. There are no rules to the Red Path, only a guideline: Be *with* the world, a part of its breath and pulse. Don't separate from wildlife and nature, be a part of them and be silent enough to learn their way and understand.

As a child, I learned our heritage had to be secretive, as my mother would chide, "We do not tell people we are Indian! It's a social distinction that we don't need. Besides, we are more European than Indian, and I don't want people thinking we're 'that kind.'" My brother and sister looked the European part, but I was dark-skinned, with dark brown eyes, and had an ability and a need to commune with animals and land. I spent any free part of a day sitting in the trees waiting for birds or raccoons or deer to get close. I watched what frightened them and what they liked to be near, logging each tiny detail, like parts of a book I hoped never to finish.

By the time I got to college, I wrote a paper about how some Chinook salmon had taught me to process grief. My professor told me I had been given a "gift" from God—she meant her Christian god, but I got the message. The Creator had infused me with an abiding love and understanding of creatures and the land. I became a photographer and worked with wildlife, spending months with elk herds, getting to know who was the lead, when it was rut season, watching them throw rainbows of light into the mist when they shook their coats steaming with morning sun. I honed my love for raccoons, bear, and deer, as well as raptors, corvids, and songbirds: only they knew me.

In my late thirties, I became a tribal liaison and got to know the nine nations within Oregon. By then, I had lived with the Hopi and Navajo, gone to powwows, potlatches, and sweats. But I was neither white nor Indian, though I could pass for either. Whites seemed to like to visit the land, like camping, rather than live in its palm with permanence. Indians had tribal affiliations and rituals only members took part in. I didn't belong wholly to either one. I returned to college and met Merle. He'd been raised on Blackfeet Nation and was struggling in school. I became his tutor, and we worked together for two years to get him to graduation. He became my confidant, my friend, and opened the door again to tribal ways.

"Woman! You got to get out to my camp. Come to Browning," he announced after graduation.

I sighed heavily, answering, "You know, a Nez Perce with half-assed blood quantum isn't going to fit in your country. I love you, Merle, but I don't want to create any issues for you on your own home turf."

"Bullshit! You're scared of belonging," he countered.

We'd have this argument every other month for about two years. Sometimes the themes varied a bit. "You got no identity because you won't claim it!" he'd bellow.

"I can't claim it—I'm not going to be one of those white people who co-opt what they like about Native Ways, then live in a way that isn't the Red Path."

"What's it going to take for you to own yourself?"

"A name," I said and he fell silent. "I know, I know. I'm not enough to enroll, not a member, so a name isn't possible." I looked away from him and finished, "I don't have an identity, my brother."

When I was in my mid-forties, Merle became ill with a lung condition, and I visited him in Browning, to the Blackfeet Nation. As predicted, I wasn't well received at first, because historically strangers had only brought trouble. Over time, connections with Dale Notafraid, Bonnie Fourowls, Elizabeth Ironmaker, and the Stillsmoking family grew and deepened. It became an easy comfort to be with them, and dinners with fry bread became a ritual. By the time we'd all gotten to where they had entered my spirit like wind on skin, it was time to return to Oregon. Merle was driving me in his truck and said we had a stop to make at George and Hummingbird Stillsmoking's place on the way to the airport. I felt like I had "arrived home" here, so I was in no hurry to leave. I remember that day as though I were living it in the moment.

I amble out toward the split-rail fence that meets the prairie, so the men can talk. They don't ask me to leave, I am simply not part of whatever they have to say. I pass stunning copper sculptures of wind catchers that dot the storied geography of the prairie. I know George's wife, Hummingbird, is an artist, and I wonder if she made them. There are two nearby teepees I saunter past before I cross over the split rail. The air has switched to September, so the dry dust of summer intermingles with the crispness of autumn as I take a deep breath of prairie.

I can see ponies in the distance, galloping, playing, and kicking up dust with the Rocky Mountains as their backdrop. I look up, hoping to get a glimpse of Brother Hawk, but am not disappointed when all that is there is the yawning Montana sky with broad strokes of blue and dabs of white. The sky has a voice of its own, alternately singing and whispering with its wind currents. Facing each one of the Directions, I send my thanks and gratitude for the ballast of this day and the soaring of these people. I am standing on the sacred ground of the Blackfeet Nation and both are filling my spirit.

I feel it and hear it at the same time—the ground rumbling and a distant thunder pounding closer. The movement catches my eye, and my focus whips to the small herd of ponies galloping directly at me with startling speed. A quick glance tells me I am too far from the house to outrun them and there is no bush, tree, or object to hide behind—I know when animals get in a pack, their behavior can become aggressive. I decide at once: I will treat them as the elk back home and drop my shoulders, arms, and head, the passive stance that lets them know I am not a threat. I ask Mother Earth to rise up through my feet and still me, slow my heart, fill me with oxygen, and dissolve my fear; she infuses me with calm. The thunder hammers the ground around me, filling the air first with sound, then with clouds of dust tanning the surroundings as the horses grind to a bumping, colliding halt in front of me. I am trying not to breathe in the dust clouds and gently hold my passive stance. A white pony with brown spots and mane pushes his muzzle against my sternum, so that I can feel his hot breath shoot out his nostrils through my shirt. Instinct tells me not to raise my hand. I use my body weight to lightly push back and rub his face with my torso; he snorts, raising his head, slowly backing up a few steps. They take turns checking me out: some of them shoving others, some coming up to me and pulling up a head or shaking a mane. I don't move. There is some hoof stomping and shifting, then as suddenly as they arrived, one rears up, sending the signal that it is time to leave. They all shift and whinny, and their trot becomes a gallop as they take their leave.

I dare to raise my head and allow my heart to resume the normal speed it had been suppressing. I watch the ponies race and romp into the prairie before I turn to go back. A shriek echoes across the sky as I near the house and my heart fills with its song—it's Brother Falcon, messaging I am to get comfortable with my own power. This makes me smile.

Inside the house, the woodstove is going. George and Merle summon me; George has sage in his hand. He begins chanting, "*Hey o hey o hee-ah, hey hey A ah, hey A o hi.*"

I don't know the words, but I do know any variation of "hey ah" is spiritual praise, so I think we must be in prayer. George continues to chant and crumble sage on the woodstove, which sparks and smokes. Suddenly I feel George's hand on my head—it's an unusual gesture, since Indian men are generally not tactile with communication, but I don't move. He announces, "Motai Auksi Piksi Ahki. That is your name. Wear it with honor."

I am chilled and feel heat at the same time, but am also speechless.

Before I can ask questions, George turns around and leaves the room. My head is spinning, but I cannot process. Merle walks toward the door, saying, "Okay, let's go." I follow numbly, but once in the pickup, I ask, "What just happened?"

For the first time, Merle breaks out in a big smile and hands me a piece of paper. "Better learn how to say it. It's your Blackfeet name."

My head is thrumming, and it makes no sense to me. "B-but I can't be named; I'm not enrolled. I—I don't understand." For a person to be named, they must have enough tribal blood quantum to enroll.

"Tribal Council held a special meeting last night. I told them about the years of work you've done for our people and that you're not eligible to enroll. They wanted to gift you. I told them your only wish was to be named, but you understood it could not be done." He pauses, turning the truck in a wide, sweeping arc and continues, "They voted to let George Stillsmoking decide, because all names go through him, and that's why we came here today."

Apart from the clattering truck sounds, we rode in silence for a bit. It began to hit me, and my eyes welled up as full as my heart. "I have a name," I whispered.

Merle gestured to the paper. "It means 'Ocean Bird Woman.' George liked that you showed respect. But when you went out to the prairie, we watched from the windows. I saw the wild ponies charging you and gunned my feet toward the door to get you out of there. George stopped me and said, 'She has a gift—I can feel it. Watch. She is safe.' Sure enough, they stopped, and you held your own. He asked for the Guides right then to send your name. Motai Auksi Piksi Ahki."

"They were wild? I—I didn't know that." I exhale and swallow that reality. "Could they have killed me or harmed me?"

Merle says flatly, "Doesn't matter, does it? They didn't."

"I have a name," I repeat dumbly. Breaking into a smile, I say it out loud for the first time, "Motai Auksi Piksi Ahki."

I think of Merle, George and Hummingbird Stillsmoking, and the others from the Blackfeet Nation with heartfelt fondness. I listen to the Pacific Ocean's rhythm and feel the cadence of the Tillamook forest. In these moments of resting in the world's palm, I can breathe. Just as I look up, I see Eagle fly over my home and call out my name, *Ocean Bird Woman*.

EVERY TIME I SEE THAT SPAM EMAIL

Poem by Amy Miller

I think of dancing with you in that Dallas
disco that I always get mixed up with the ball-
shaped restaurant that rotated, spilling a view
from Mesquite to Fort Worth, or maybe we were in
some underground mall that night. I do know
the music was loud and the place as empty
as a bar could be in that boomtown cowtown in 1980,
and my hands after twenty minutes smelled like your
cologne even though we hardly touched. And I had
the mother of all colds and a voice like Bob Marley
and the week of my first business trip had all
caught up with me right then. And even though
you were from the Emirates and I'd looked forward
to this night for months since we'd met by telex—
remember: our fingers pressing in turn on a series
of keys that whispered through lines deep under
the ocean—even though when you finally arrived
on a trip to buy helicopters for a prince—yes,
this was real, this was not some con—when we finally met,
you were younger and thinner and more like a college kid
than I'd pictured, and who knows what you thought
of me—I have no clear memory of myself that young,
a dream of sheer paper, dress like a twisted
candy wrapper. And I went back to the chilled dark
of my hotel room alone, I could not stand to be awake
with that headache a minute more, and I was a terrible
date, germs and coughing and strangled talk
and dancing in a drugged half-sleep. And now
every time I see that spam email I think maybe,

maybe it's you who's died and left me three million
seven hundred forty-six thousand dollars for the lonely
spark of one night, and the lawyer who says he represents
the dearly deceased is really your uncle in Dubai
who's found me after months of tracking, a man
at a sunlit desk, just back from lunch with a woman
he hopes to marry, a widow he met in a neighbor's yard
made gloriously cool by a dome of Bougainvillea, a woman
whose hand he let go of an hour ago to hover over
a gray keyboard and type me the end of this story.

HOW TO BEHAVE IN SEWING

Nonfiction by Ruth Leibowitz

I should not talk during sewing. Talking may annoy other people.

Another reason not to talk is that we won't be able to hear the records, and other people like the music. I might also get extra homework if I talk.

I should also not walk around or go to other people's desks, like I did last week. I should not turn around to look at someone else's work or their face.

If I have to borrow something to do my work, I should ask the teacher first. I should not be doing anything except tracing the pattern, pinning, cutting, or sewing.

I should know when to use a thimble. Otherwise I might get a hole in my skin. It could get infected and I might die of sepsis like my daddy's brother after he fell on a fence.

I especially should pay attention when you, the teacher, are showing us a new skill that requires eye-hand coordination. If we don't learn these skills right, someone could sew her fingers together, or sew her hand to a different part of her body where it doesn't belong.

I shouldn't whisper across the room or even move my mouth.

I must be careful not even to look as though I'm chewing, winking, or any of those other things that show bad self-control. I should not make faces, pop my cheeks, snap my fingers, stamp my feet, etc. I should also not dance, since that is a different class that I like very much.

If I look out the window and see a flying saucer land right outside our school, and then green and orange creatures with ray guns climb out, I should keep my observations to myself. That has nothing to do with our class and might disturb the other students or distract you, the teacher.

These are the ways I know I should behave during sewing.

I want it to be known, though, that I was not allowed to take the shop class and was forced to take this class.

I didn't say a word to anyone but you, the teacher, during sewing period today, and I don't think you should make everyone write a composition like this since they didn't do anything wrong, they just didn't tell on me for doing things I shouldn't. I don't think it's fair to punish the whole class for me being the way I am.

Of course, this is just my opinion, and I hope you don't get angry and make me leave the class.

Yours Very Truly,

Grace Sparks
Class 5-330
May 2, 1967

COOKIE SEASON

Nonfiction by Sarah Mott

One hundred boxes of Thin Mints. Nine year-old Maria makes a checkmark on the inventory sheet then quickly stows it back in her jacket before it gets wet. *Two hundred boxes of Samoas.* It's spring in Portland, and unusually rainy for a city that's already perpetually damp. *One hundred twenty boxes of Trefoils.* We've set up our booth at the corner of Macadam Avenue and Taylor's Ferry Road, outside the local Zupan's Market. This particular Zupan's is a fixture in Southwest Portland, and a nexus for snobby delicatessens, devotees of strange and exotic diets, and connoisseurs of local brews. Basically, everyone in the city. It's also the very toughest assignment for a cookie booth.

Seventy-five boxes of Tagalongs. In a place that prides itself in the unconventional, nothing is more orthodox-all-American, and therefore gauche, than a box of Girl Scout Cookies. Especially when sold by a detachment of uniformed agents. Being hardened veterans of cookie season, however, my troop of nine-year-old scouts is well-prepared for any quirk or eccentricity the southwest borough has to offer.

…and twenty-five Smores. Maria makes her final checkmark, then nods up at me. The rest of the girls spread out around the booth, giggling and concocting silly dances to catch the attention of local shoppers.

"Seriously, how can you let them sell these things?" A thin blonde woman in $300 yoga pants grabs a box of thin mints and waves them in my face. "These are loaded with saturated fat!"

"Actually," says trooper Andrea from beside me, pushing up her horn-rimmed glasses, "a moderate amount of saturated fat supports digestive health and improves immunity. But we also accept direct donations." She gestures toward a tin can on the table. With an apologetic smile, I shrug and point to Andrea. The woman storms off in a huff, slamming the box of cookies down on the table.

"Goodbye! Thank you," choruses the troop.

"How do you know all that stuff?" Maria whispers to Andrea, who shrugs and hands the mangled box to me.

"Collateral damage." I say in a grievous tone. "We'll not let this one die in vain." I tear open the damaged box, then an individual tube of the Girl Scouts' flagship cookie. The troop moves in on the open pack like a group of wild hyenas. I quickly pull one free, narrowly missing the loss of a finger.

"Hey, what are you guys selling?" A man with a dancing bear on his T-shirt wobbles up to the table. His friend, wearing dark sunglasses in ten inches of rain, leans over to inspect the multi-color boxes.

"Cookies!" The girls chorus, now full of all-American chocolate.

"Whoa!" The man's blood-shot eyes widen momentarily. "What should I get?"

"These Thin Mints are really good" says Janoi, pulling a cookie from the tube to hand to him.

"Dude, you guys should not be eating from your own stash." I snort, and the girls stare at me quizzically. "I'll take ten—no," he turns to his friend. "How many should we get, twenty? We'll take twenty boxes." The girls cheer at the unusually large sale and pack the boxes into a cardboard crate.

"Goodbye! Thank you," they chorus as the two stagger back to their car.

A woman who had been waiting in line behind them steps up to the table. Leaning forward, she stares at the pin that my brunette daughter wears on her uniform: *Orgullosa de ser una Girl Scout*. She quickly glances around to find a girl who definitely speaks English, but all of them wear identical buttons. "I WOULD LIKE…ONE BOX OF THIN MINTS PLEASE!" She shouts at my daughter in measured syllables to make sure she understands English, her first language. Maria leans over to her "*¿Ella es sorda?*"

"*No lo sé*" she responds and hands her the box, grinning taking her five dollars in return. The troop yells "Goodbye! Thank you!"

An older gentleman with a cane hobbles up to the front of the line, greeting the girls as he pursues the cookie selection. "How are you, sir?" I smile over at him.

"Cute group of girls." He says, smiling.

"So they are."

"Tell me," he says, apropos of nothing, "what do you think of those girls joining the Boy Scouts?"

"The Boy Scouts?" Alarm bells start going off in my head. How should I respond to this in front of the girls?

"Yeah, the girls…and they're not even boys. Why are they doing that?"

"Well, the Boy Scouts are really a different organization from ours. They're not just the *boy* version of us…"

Impatient, the man cuts me off. Turning to the girls, he fires off the same question. Larger alarm bells go off in my head. How can I diffuse this situation in the calmest, kindest way possible?

"What do *you* think about girls joining the Boy Scouts?" he asks the girls.

The girls look back and forth at each other momentarily. "Boys are stupid." Maria replies. The others nod their heads in solidarity.

The man nods in concession and buys five Thin Mints before hobbling away.

"Goodbye! Thank you," yells the troop.

A week earlier, the troop sat cross-legged on the carpet in a ring we call the "Brownie circle." This holistic, top-down planning method predates Kaizen by thirty years and requires zero PowerPoint slides and zero M.B.A.s. Yet somehow, a group of ten people (albeit nine-year-old people) are able to identify an issue, mutually agree on a solution, and plan for all the logistics and administration.

In a matter of thirty minutes.

My co-leader and I glance at each other amazed as the girls discuss the upcoming cookie sales. Each one voices her idea. The others wait quietly until the speaker is finished, then discuss the idea in turns. *Seriously, is it healthy for kids to be this well-mannered and thoughtful?* I make a note to have an extemporaneous dance party at the end of the meeting…just in case.

"OK, I think that we're ready to start selling cookies next week." My co-leader claps her hands together in a signal that it's time to wrap up. "What questions do you guys have?"

"Can we hand out business cards?" "Can I bring my dog?" "Can we eat the cookies we don't sell?" "Do we have to sell cookies to Boy Scouts?" "Is it going to rain?"

"Next week? No, I don't think so," I say, quickly checking my phone's weather app. "Are there any other questions? About anything else?" The girls grin. This open-ended question period at the end of the circle has become an absurd and zany ritual for the group.

"Can you give a girl cat a boy name?"

"Yes," I say. Easy one.

"Can I go to Mars?"

"Yes."

"Can I go tomorrow?"

"No. Next question"

"Can turtles really breath out of their butts?"

"You know…I think they actually can."

"Can dogs be an American?" asks Maria.

"Yes, dogs can be American."

"My dog's a German Shepherd," offers one of the other girls.

Maria persists, "No, I mean can a dog be an American like we can. Can a dog vote for president?"

"No, a dog cannot be an American citizen."

"Why not?" The Troop stares at me, honestly concerned about this new development.

"Uhm…. Because dogs would vote for the candidate with the most treats." The girls giggle.

"That's true," says Janoi, a recent transplant from Kenya. "I heard

Donald Trump has no dog. So probably he has no treats to offer." The girls giggle. My co-leader gives me a silent signal. We try to avoid political issues as much as possible.

"OK, guys," I cut in. "Let's sing some songs. Who has a song we can all sing?"

"I heard that Donald Trump doesn't like immigrants. Is that true?" my own daughter cuts in.

"This is not a discussion for right now." I use my teacher-voice. "This is a discussion for you and your parents."

"But I heard that he puts them in cages like you put pets in cages." Annie, one of the smallest troopers cuts in.

Andrea breaks in. "He puts them in cages, and he takes them away from their mom and dad."

A horrified hush settles over the room. I glance at my co-leader who looks back at me with alarm. Janoi looks down at her sneakers silently. *As a parent, you find that there are times where it's necessary to skirt the truth with kids.*

"My mam's an immigrant. Are they going to take my mam away from me?" Maria is trying to sound angry, but her face is pale. My heart sinks. *As a parent, you find that there are also times that you cannot skirt truth with kids.* The troop stares at me with expectation. I don't know what the right thing is to do here. What am I supposed to say? I'm not an immigrant. I'm not even part of an underserved community. I know nothing about policy, and nothing about immigration law.

"No," I say loudly, confidently at Maria, then I turn to Janoi. "No one is taking any of you away from your parents. There are lots of people who care about you and we will not let that happen. You are all safe." I kick myself inwardly. I don't know that any of that is true. But the girls noticeably relax and look around at each other. Color starts to return to their faces.

"But it's true that this is happening to some kids. If this is something you are worried about, there are things that you can do. Whenever you are worried about something that is happening, you can do things that will make a difference, even if you're a kid." I take in a couple breaths, trying not to be too obvious. "One thing we could do is to donate part of our cookie money to a group that will help those kids. I know that we all decided to put the money toward camp, but maybe we could donate the extra to a group that's working to free those kids and reunite them with their families."

"Could we donate all of it?" says Annie. The other girls murmur in agreement. "I want to go to camp, but I want to help those kids more than that."

I put my hand over my eyes, which are quickly tearing. My co-leader takes over, "Who votes that we donate all of our cookie sale money to a non-profit that helps immigrant children at the boarder?" The vote is unanimous. We will now spend our money on helping other kids. Good job you guys! That is really thoughtful of you."

During the subsequent dance party, the kids spin around joyfully—ecstatic at their new-found power to create change. I spin around too, humbled by the moment. How could I ever think that volunteering would be a wasteful drag on my time—an inexcusable distraction from my career? This is where the nuts and bolts of community are. Working with kids is absolutely the best way to learn about being a human, and how we all fit together.

It's two months later, and cookie season has ended. The troop sits around a long, two-sided table in the Oregon Girl Scout Headquarters. The girls are pleased with their accomplishment, having raised significant funds for several non-profits and still managing to get into camp that spring via an anonymous donor.

I shout a few times and wave my arms to get their attention. "Alright crew, you guys did a fantastic job. We exceeded all our cookie goals, including my calorie-intake goal. You have a right to be proud of yourselves! You worked hard and did something truly selfless. That makes you guys really special. Sooooo…." I click on the projector and a PowerPoint slide appears. The girls groan at a prospect of a presentation. "Nope! No no no…listen up. I think it's time we distinguished ourselves as a very special troop. Who knows what distinguished means?"

Zoey raises her hand "It's when you are different. But in a good way."

"First of all, being different is always in a good way," I retort. "Second, yes you are absolutely right. Good job." I click the next slide, which shows several examples of Girl Scout-approved crests. "There are two hundred approved crests for troops to choose to represent themselves…unicorn, rabbit, tiger. I think we should make up our own."

The group stares at me aghast. Adia, one of the troopers, raises her hand, "Is that against the rules?"

"I don't know. Let's do it!" The girls whisper amongst each other, concerned. My co-leader smirks. We hand out pieces of paper to each of the ten girls. "Now I want each of you to write down what you would like to see on your very-unique troop crest. Don't show anyone yet." Each girl thinks for several minutes before writing down her choice. They giggle and whisper among themselves as they hand in their papers. There are, interestingly enough, four cats, five dogs, and one sloth among the nominations. The Dog Party cheers as I write the results up on the white board.

"Not so fast! We're going to do something called *ranked choice voting*. Who knows what that is?" The room stares back at me silently. "Everyone is going to get a new piece of paper, and you are going to write down your first, second, and third choice."

This round of voting reveals 42% support for a dog crest, 38% for sloths, and the remainder for cats. This time, the dog supporters are weary of cheering pre-emptively. "Now," I say, after recording the results, "You all have ten minutes to try and convince your fellow Girl Scouts to vote with you. Ready go!"

At first, no one speaks. They look around at each other quizzically. Then, almost at once, each girl turns to her neighbor and starts discussing the vote. Voting blocks are quickly formed. Friends are pulled across party lines. Bribery of all kinds takes place: from stickers, to markers, to diamonds and emeralds on Minecraft.

Factions within the groups form. The kids move to different sides of the table according to their vote. The sloth party offers the cat party a tiny cat icon on the crest alongside the sloth, if they join their vote. Two kids change their minds and shouting starts between the groups. My co-leader and I glance at each other, concerned. *Should we stop this experiment now before it damages the cohesion of the troop?*

Young Janoi breaks up the fight. The kids return to their respective sides of the table and whisper amongst themselves. A similar offer is made to the cat supporters from the dog party. At last, the timer goes off on my iPhone and the huddles on either side break up and return to their seats.

"OK everyone, last vote. We are going to have one more ranked vote. The animal we decide on will be featured in our new troop crest." My co-leader and I double count and calculate the results while the troop stares on, uncharacteristically quiet.

"And the winner by a hair, *a hair of the dog,* are the dogs!" The dog voters jump up from their seats and cheer, while the other half of the room groans unhappily. I click the next slide on the projector which reads "SNACK TIME" and turn around to dig out the snacks from our troop box.

After a short, awkward silence, one of the troopers leans forward and asks her friend across the table, "Hey, did you name your cat Jason?"

"Yeah," she responds, a bit discomfited. "But then we took him to the vet and found out he was really a girl." The whole room giggles.

"Hey, can I use your purple marker?" another girl asks from across the table.

"Sure," says the other, pulling it out of her bag.

Conversation begins again, resplendent with jokes and giggles and impressions and war stories from various video games. The girls are friends again. I grin, amazed at was has happened. *You guys don't know how democracy works,* I want to tell them sardonically. Biting into a cupcake, I think about where we as a people have been the last couple of years: all the hatred, the name-calling, the blocking, the unfriending.

There is so much we can learn from these children, from these *young people*, before they have the chance to be corrupted by the forces that have pulled us all apart.

I begin to tear up again, and my co-leader hands me another cupcake. I bite into it just as my daughter bites into hers. She looks up at me and smiles. Maybe it's this generation. Maybe they're just a bit better than we are or, hopefully, much better. Maybe the next one will be better still and that's something to hold on to and look forward to. And to learn from.

Every cookie season, I see the same group of ordinary Portlanders waiting in line to buy cookies from our booth. But the kids still see the bizarre and unusual nature of each individual. They learn to accept differences, work with differences long before they learn to be afraid of them. They are essential teachers to us right now, while all this is happening. We need only take the time to sit down, cross-legged, and listen. Really listen.

PART III

MY GRANDMA'S ESSAY TO THE AMERICAN SCHOOL PEACE LEAGUE*
JULY 1912

Poem by Suzy Harris

When the war is over, Europe must not go out
imbued with the idea that might makes right.
What is it then, what can we do?
The life of a nation endangered, trouble begins.
People are anxious for peaceful relations.
Draw up a peace not for the victor and the conquered,

but a peace of humanity, of justice, of equality.
Not until nations respect the rights of each other
can we hope for universal peace.
Women are women, and stronger than the tie of race,
is like to like. These women bear the brunt of the war
in their common sorrow—not the type of old
who "grieved they had no more sons
to give their country," these were educated,
thinking women of the 20th century who realized
that if they are to have a government
for the people, their voice must be felt.
Women do not shut their eyes to the conditions of the world.
We must not sit idly by waiting for the war to end.

---

*This is a found poem—all words are from a three-page handwritten essay my grandmother Hermien Danenbaum Nusbaum submitted to American School Peace League contest when she was 17. (It was kindly rejected.) The words are in the same order as they appear in the essay (and stanzas reflect paragraphs) but much has been deleted, sentences fragments have been formed into new sentences, and capitalization and punctuation have been changed in some places.

GREENIE

Fiction by Gabriel Granillo

Mother's house is much more modest than mine, but it feels more homey. I don't know what it is.

Maybe it's because she's always got a bowl of Hershey's Kisses on the kitchen table, or maybe it's because it always smells like coffee and sage. Maybe it's that old Maine Coon, lavishly adorned with a brown and grey coat, strips of white like trails of a falling star. She waltzes around the garden all majestic, moving like a queen as basil and thyme and rosemary, delicate like feathers, brush against her flowing hair. Fancy Cat we call her.

Maybe it's the way the afternoon sun hits the living room window just right. You can see dust and tiny hairs floating like flowers. Maybe it's just Mother. But no matter what I do, no matter what memories I've attached to my place out in Vineleaf, no matter how perfect the view of Ranana Peak, no matter what color drapes I find, what candle I burn, how bright or how clean, how quiet or how distinct, how floral and fun, that house is just a house, where I sleep. Home will always be at Mother's. And she lives on Herbert Hill.

It's a little purple two-bedroom home that she insists was built in the nineteen-forties, although last year she told me it was from the fifties, and the year before that it was the thirties, so I'm not sure what to believe anymore. Dad would probably know. He was a handyman of sorts, interested in architecture, history, and the Dodgers. He died twelve years ago from kidney failure. I remember because David and I had decided, just before we received the call from Mother, that we would get a divorce. It couldn't have been more than ten or fifteen minutes before Mother called, crying and laughing, telling me that Dad's last words were, "I think I left the oven on." David and I had a sad laugh about it, too, and then went our separate ways.

Mother moved into the purple house about a year after Dad died, and I started seeing Yung. He was the construction inspector for the city of Tulip, where I was, and still am, a city planner—at least until next month. I liked beer and he liked wine. I liked horror and he liked romance. He looked like Johnny Cash and I like June. And like most of Johnny Cash's songs, this one ended much too soon. Yung and I are currently going through a divorce. As a result, I have accepted a position as a public works supervisor in Culver City, California.

I haven't told Mother any of this, but I suspect she figures something. She keeps giving me glances from beyond her reading glasses, scrolling up and up through her newsfeed on her tablet as we wait for Dizzy. I wonder if she's actually reading anything.

Typically, Mother's house is as quiet as a museum, but today a Roomba is buzzing around and Mother's Assistant is playing Dave Koz. It's indiscreet enough, but I'm not in the mood for smooth sax today. I just want Dizzy to get here so we can see whatever movie Mother has decided we should see.

Dizzy's my younger brother by five years, and Mother's youngest and only boy. Dad would always say something like "You're my favorite son" before laughing about it for days. It was cute, and I still say things like "You're my favorite brother" because it reminds me of him.

"Greenie," my mother says. "It's so good to see you. How's Yung?"

How's *Yung*. "He's fine," I say.

"You doing okay?"

"I'm fine. Just anxious to get to the movies. When's Dizzy getting here?"

After asking the question, the top of Mother's Assistant shines a blue light and says, "Dizzy is approximately sixteen minutes from Mama Maple's Motel." The light dims and the silver cylinder looks like a metal pole. Iris we call her.

I ask, "Did you really name your home location Mama Maple's Motel?"

"It's cute isn't it? It's for the Air BnBers."

"Wait, when did you start doing that?"

"About four months ago. I told you," she says. "It's great. Most people just crash for the night and are gone before I come back from capoeira," Mother takes off her glasses and throws her hands in the air, *look on my works, ye mighty*. "And it gives me some extra money for travel and all this cool stuff."

The Roomba buzzes about the hardwood floor, hits the coffee table leg, and then redirects itself around the couch.

"Hey, Iris." Mother sinks back on the couch, puts on her glasses, and continues to scroll through her feed. Iris' blue eye shines like a beacon, listening for the transmission. "Text Dizzy: Just honk twice when you get here. We'll come out. Love you. Smiley face.'"

Something about this makes no sense to me, as if texting could be any more impersonal, now we're telling little chrome monoliths to do it for us. I must be making a scowl or twisting my face or who knows what because Mother is shaking her head.

"Oh, don't give me that," she says.

I get up from Mother's cream-colored couch and make my way to the window overlooking the front lawn. A man on a motorized skateboard zooms by on the sidewalk and drops his travel cup, but he doesn't notice. As he nods his head to the beat of whatever song is blasting on his headphones, the cup rolls down the hill, clink-clanking against the sidewalk until it disappears. I wonder when he'll notice, *if* he'll notice. Maybe he's got another one at home. Maybe that wasn't even his. Maybe he'll go through the rest of his life without ever wondering what happened to that cup, what became of his old friend.

Is that all we are? Cups rolling down into oblivion? There's a poem here. Something to be said about discarding people like objects when we're done loving and hating each other. Maybe I'll write it in a book someday. Yung would laugh at the thought. He felt art belonged to artists, not city planners and construction inspectors. I wrote him a poem one time, and he said to me, "Neat. I love the imagery." The last resort of someone who has nothing to say about art. He never brought it up ever again. He never asked about my poems or what they meant. I was a well of unexpressed thought, wishing for him to ask for a drink. He did once ask me why I wrote such silly things, and I told him because it was something I felt, something had told me to. He didn't understand. I barely do.

I don't hate Yung, and he doesn't hate me—I don't think—but we don't love each other anymore. We just fell out of love, and there's something more painful in that, something that makes me think there's something fundamentally wrong with me. Something internal that can't be fixed. Some pre-existing condition. A broken travel mug.

The wind blows like winter, but the sun feels like summer. Mother's herb garden seems lonely and dead, and I say, "Haven't seen Fancy Cat in a while."

"Yeah, she hasn't been coming around lately."

Mother takes a spot by my side and together we listen to the wind push through barren trees, blowing their fallen leaves along the streets. It's just the wind and Mother and me, and it's so quiet I can hear a train rumbling through downtown.

"I think it's getting too cold for her," she says.

"Well, if it's getting too cold for me, it's probably too cold for Fancy Cat." My hands feel cold, and my feet feel cold, and, *my god*, why am I always so cold? Coffee sounds great, so I ask for some. Mother gives me a look. Before she says anything I know she doesn't have any.

"I started drinking Yerba Mate," she says. "Maybe we can pick some up on the way to the movie."

"It's fine. What movie are we watching anyway?"

Iris' blue glow gleams over my mother's shoulder and her greying hair, and she speaks.

"The movie is called *Second Storm*. Directed by J.B. Ives, and starring Lucy Lampross and Gavin Prebble, the film explores the romantic relationship between two lovers post-World War II."

Her voice is soft and soothing, and it reminds me of Aunt Clara when she drinks too much. Aunt Clara gets all smooth, and she sings like a desperate poet searching for something of importance to say.

When I look up at Mother, she's glued to her tablet again, reading some story about social media data mining that she found on Twitter. The irony is glaringly obvious, staring at me the way that little camera on Mother's tablet stares at her, the way Iris' little blue eye stares at her. Mother seems frail and content, lost inside that brave new world she's crawled in to. Where do I fit inside her retired, spouseless, Yerba-Mate-filled life? Somewhere. I know I'm in there. Somewhere, me and Dizzy, but she doesn't even have the time to text Dizzy or answer my stupid question about this stupid movie herself. Iris does. Pretty soon she'll sprout arms and give us a hug, that bitch.

"Iris," I say, "please shut up."

Mother acts as though I've insulted the pope or kicked a kitten. "Hey." Mother cuts in between me and Iris as if we're about to start a fist fight. "Don't talk to Iris like that."

"Jesus Christ, Mother, Iris is just a piece of rebar."

"She's not just some inanimate object, Greenie."

"No," I say. "She's a silver dildo that talks and consumes and analyzes your behavior for advertising companies and Russian hackers."

"*Greenie*, good lord." Mother takes a seat on the couch, her hand against her chest and her mouth agape.

Greenie. *Greenie*. I think of my brown eyes and my brown hair and my white skin that turns red, as it is now, whenever I get flustered or angry, and my forever-conscious decision to avoid the color green because of that god-forsaken name. Greenie. *What kind of a name is that?* After forty-two years, I finally decide to ask her.

I take a step backward as Mother's Roomba makes another lap around my legs. It sideswipes me, and I tumble on to the floor. The fall is less serious than the thunderous thrashing against the wooden floor implies, but Mother shrieks. She tells Iris to stop the music, runs over, almost falling herself, and mumbles nonsense as she checks to see if I'm all right. I remember someone once told me that you know you're getting old when it's no longer funny when you fall.

I know I'm getting older, but I feel like I'm three, looking at Mother for the appropriate reaction to make here. Please laugh, Mother. But she doesn't. And I start to cry.

"Greenie, are you OK?" Mother says, combing my hair. "What's happening? Should I call Yung?"

Good lord, can't she stop asking me about Yung? *Good lord*, I sound like Mother.

It's both a blessing and a curse that when you're involved with anybody you become irrevocably attached to them, how much of who you are and who they are becomes one entity, so that when you're at a dinner party or a Sunday social or a visit to your mother's house, the first thing anyone asks is, "How's Yung?" Even you get lost in it, twirling around each other in some grand sense of togetherness. Everything you do becomes based on the idea of a greater good. There's something comforting and terrifying about that.

"No, Mother," I say. "I'm fine. It just hurt is all."

"It's more than that," she says.

"Can we talk about it some other time?" Mother's cool palm cradles my face. I stop crying about as fast as I started, and I close my eyes and sit inside memories of that comfort, that literal hand helping subdue the pain. After breaking my nose when I slammed against the garage door on my bike or when Grandma Oakley died. Mother's hand was always there. I'll miss it when I move.

"Is it Yung?" she asks.

I say nothing and wipe tears against my shoulder. Mother hugs me. She knows. I can feel it in the way she massages my back. We say nothing, holding each other in the stillness of the purple home, the Roomba done sweeping and the train done rumbling and the wind done blowing. Something compels me to talk about the job in Culver City. Before I can speak, two horns sound off outside the door.

"Was that sixteen minutes already?" Mother asks.

"I don't think even Iris could account for how fast Dizzy drives." I chuckle, wiping my eyes and face as to not arise awkward suspicion from Dizzy. He wouldn't know what to do. He gets that from Dad.

"I guess not." Mother looks into my eyes and says, "When you're ready, you can talk to me about anything you want. My mother, I didn't always feel like I could speak to her. I always felt like I had to do things on my own. I just want to you feel like you can talk to me. If you can't right now, that's all right. Let's just watch a movie, and we can talk about it later. That sound good?"

She helps me up and gives me another hug.

"I love you, Greenie," she says, and that name hits me again. *Good lord.*

Mother runs around me, grabs our purses, and hands me mine. As she starts for the door I finally ask her.

"Why did you name me Greenie?"

Mother looks at me with a confidence I have never in my life seen this woman elicit, as if she had been waiting all of my forty-two years for me to ask this question, and says, "because you looked like the color green."

She starts back for the door, and Dizzy honks two more times.

"Wait, what?" I say. "I looked like the color green, so you named me Greenie? What kind of an answer is that? What, did you feel a little woozy when you had your son so you named him Dizzy?"

She laughs. I needed that a little earlier, Mother.

"No. Like Gillespie," she says.

I sigh and try again. "In what way, Mother, did I look like the color green to you?"

"I don't know. I just looked into your big ol' eyes—"

"My big ol' *brown* eyes," I say.

"I just looked into your big ol' brown eyes and, I don't know, you just felt green. Your father and I had just moved to Tulip. It was spring, and I had never seen so much green in my life. It just felt right at the time. Something told me to. Goodbye, Iris."

"Goodbye," Iris says. As her blue eye fades away into a rainbow of colors, she plays a three-note descending tune to which Mother whistles.

There is so much about her I do not understand, an entire life before me and Dizzy, before Dad, before the purple house. Has she always felt this warmly about life? Has she always greeted it like a child, with a hug and smile, blind to all the bullshit—Sorry, Mother. I was made of Mother's eyes that look at me with love beyond that which I can possibly handle. As a child I was cradled in her arms, bathed by her hands, carried by her legs, and supported by her back as I grew and grew inside her belly, wreaking havoc on and taking from her body. Sometimes I worry life is made up of only two types of people: those who take and those who get taken from.

I am here, following Mother out the door, watching the sunlight cast a golden glow across her back, because of some intangible feeling between her and Dad, some indefinable spirit of connection I've been taught to seek, yet when I feel I've found it, it seems to slip away into oblivion. A cup rolling down a hill.

I was born of love. I was born an artist, but it just so happens I was made into a public works supervisor. Yung could tell me something practical and pragmatic about it. Some solution to my struggles as if they were so simple. I *don't* hate Yung. I hate how there is no me without him. How do I become my own person without wondering what Yung would say or how Dad would respond or what Mother would think? I am made from all of these people, and yet I am not like any of them.

Mother opens the door, and we walk out and wave to Dizzy who's waiting with his window down. There's a rustling from the neighbor's lawn, and suddenly mother grabs my hand. She gasps and smiles as she pats my hand. Through a dried-up lantana bush, Fancy Cat emerges. The queen making her entrance.

"Hey, Fancy Cat." Dizzy waves and smiles, then looks at Mother and me, hand in hand. "Come on. The movie starts in five minutes."

Mother smiles and guides me to the car. As we drive away, Fancy Cat sneaks through a slot in the metal fence and takes her leisurely stroll through Mother's dead garden.

MOTHER'S LIFE LIST

Poem by Stephanie Striffler

Male western tanager with broken wing,
May 13, 1954.
Red-winged blackbird, three miles north of Isleta,
canyon towhee, dark-eyed junco.

Where did you rest as you entered
your pencil lines, fine as sighs,
inside the cover of Peterson's Field Guide?
As you watched out the window for flitting
in the cottonwood, you kept watch
for me, too, to stir,
curled in the tiny nest of your tummy.
Did you scan the fence line past a sinkful of dishes,
pacing on linoleum, waiting for my father,
flicking ash after ash into the basin?
By that June, the tree swallows
were swooping for damselflies,
the sunflower cell that would one day
make your granddaughter
had begun to bloom inside me,
inside you.
Red-shafted flicker, California jay.
Which call pulled you
from your long afternoon sleep?
I do not remember my first home.
Yet here I am,
the daughter you carried,
knowing the tanager flaring yellow
from belly to scarlet crown,

knowing the way your eyes cupped tears
like hummingbird eggs,
the way your heart fluttered, defeated,
to see that broken wing.

KELLY GREEN

Script by Robin E. Goldfin

First produced in the Eclectic Evening of Shorts with the ANDTheatre Company in New York in 2020.

Characters:
MARSHA: mid-30s.
JIMMY: her 8-year-old son.
JAMES: her son at 24. A soldier.

Time: Early fall, just yesterday.
Place: A public park.

AT RISE: Sounds of children playing. We see a tree, a bench, and a trashcan. MARSHA is sitting on the bench. JIMMY is close by.

MARSHA: Did you hear what I said?

JIMMY: Yes, I heard you 20 times!

MARSHA: No, you hear what you want to hear—like most men. Like suddenly, you're all grown up! What did I say, Jimmy?

JIMMY: "Don't go where I can't see you."

MARSHA: So where did you go, Jimmy?

JIMMY: No place special.

MARSHA: Stay where I can see you!

(He starts to back up, Stage Left, two steps at a time.)

JIMMY: Can you see me?

MARSHA: Yes.

JIMMY: Can you see me?

MARSHA: Yes.

(He is offstage)

JIMMY: Can you see me?

MARSHA: Don't go any farther than that! Stay right there! (Her phone rings, she answers.) Hi Mom…Jimmy and I are at the park…Yes, it's a beautiful day…STAY RIGHT THERE, JIMMY!…What? Sorry, I'm trying to keep an eye…Yes, he's getting big. He'll be nine by the time you see him in December…One Chanukah present will be enough—you didn't miss his birthday….I know. Harry would have been so proud……..No, last night didn't work out, he was a dud….No, that one was worse…….I'm not trying to find someone to measure up—and I resent—Sure, put Dad on—wait. Jimmy! I can't see you! Where did you go? Mom, I'll call you back! Jimmy—JAMES! JAMES!!!

(JAMES enters from Right.)

JAMES: I'm right here.

MARSHA: (turning to him) What?

JAMES: Don't yell. I'm right here.

MARSHA: (startled) Excuse me?

JAMES: Where you can see me.

MARSHA: I—I have to find my son. (Calling off.) Jimmy! James!! (She stars off Left) JAMES!!!

JAMES: I'm right here, Marsha. (pause) It's me, Mom.

MARSHA: Who are you?

   (He hands her his dog tags.)

MARSHA (reading): Private. James. Glass? That is not possible. What have you done with my son?!!

JAMES: I haven't done anything. It's what happens.

MARSHA: What happens?

JAMES: This.

MARSHA: You were just eight years old!

JAMES: Time flies.

MARSHA: Not like that!

JAMES: Sometimes.

MARSHA: I'm calling the police.

JAMES: They won't be able to help you.

MARSHA: How old are you?

JAMES: I'll be 25 on November 11th.

   (She grabs for her phone.)

JAMES: Who are you calling?

MARSHA: I'm not calling, I'm calculating. You've got me so *fa-mish'd* [confused], I can't think straight….8 minus 25—No, wait. You'll be 9. Then you'll be 25. Oh, God!

JAMES: In sixteen years.

MARSHA: (startled) Where did the last sixteen years go?

JAMES: I often ask myself that question.

MARSHA (Suddenly): Are you married?

JAMES: Twice.

MARSHA: I missed your weddings?

JAMES: No, you were there.

MARSHA: Your father. How long since your father—?

JAMES: When I was two. I don't really remember him. I imagine, but I don't really remember.

MARSHA: You're a soldier. Like him.

JAMES: Like him. And I'm going off again.

MARSHA: To where?

JAMES: You wouldn't believe it.

MARSHA: Where???

JAMES: Right here.

MARSHA: Why? (Realizing) War?!

JAMES: Worse.

MARSHA: What's worse than war? (Imagining) Oh, God—don't go!

JAMES: I have to.

MARSHA: Just like your father.

JAMES: Yes.

MARSHA: I couldn't stop him, either.

JAMES: No.

MARSHA: Is this a dream? Am I seeing into the future? Your future? It's like…*A Christmas Carol*, but with two unlikely Jews?!

JAMES: Could be.

MARSHA: Oh. You've grown up.

JAMES: Yes.

MARSHA: Are you happy?

JAMES: Yes. Are you?

MARSHA: Yes, I have you. But I'm a little lonely. I miss your father.

JAMES: I know.

MARSHA: Are you? Lonely?

JAMES: No. I have Kelly.

MARSHA: Kelly?

JAMES: His name is Kelly.

MARSHA: Like the color!

JAMES: Yes. Green. That's his name. Kelly Green.

MARSHA: Kelly Green?!

JAMES: His mother had a sense of humor.

MARSHA: I love Kelly Green! I love his mother! Will I meet him?

JAMES: Yes.

MARSHA: Will I meet his mother?

JAMES: Yes!

MARSHA: I'm so happy!

JAMES: I'm happy you're happy!

MARSHA: Do you still play the violin?!

JAMES: I never played the violin. I play the cello.

MARSHA: Just checking. (She kisses his forehead) You look so much like your father.

JAMES: Do I?

MARSHA: So handsome in a uniform.

JAMES: And out of one.

MARSHA: Don't get fresh!

JAMES: It makes Kelly happy.

MARSHA: Does he make you happy?

JAMES: Yes.

MARSHA: Oh, I'm so proud of you.

JAMES: I'm glad to hear you say that. (Pause) I wasn't sure.

MARSHA: Don't be ridiculous. I'm your mother.

JAMES: Thanks, I'll remember that.

(Pause. She studies him.)

MARSHA: What's wrong?

JAMES: How do you know something's wrong?

MARSHA: Remember?

   (Together)

MARSHA: I'm your mother.

JAMES: You're my mother.

JAMES: He's sick.

MARSHA: Who?

JAMES: Kelly.

MARSHA: How sick?

JAMES: I'm scared I might lose him.

MARSHA: Oh.

JAMES: (remembering) "It takes so long to find what you love in life—"

MARSHA: (finishing it) "—and then life takes it away."

JAMES: It's what you always said.

MARSHA: It's what happens.

JAMES: I don't know what's going to happen.

MARSHA: None of us do.

JAMES: I don't know if I can handle this. And I don't want to let him down.

MARSHA: You love him?

JAMES: I do.

MARSHA: You won't let him down.

JAMES: I'm losing confidence…

MARSHA: In what?

JAMES: Myself.

MARSHA: Many things on the outside can make us lose our confidence. (She puts her hand on his heart.) Only something inside can bring it back again.

(She rubs his chest gently.)

JAMES: It hurts.

MARSHA: That's how you know it's working.

(Pause)

JAMES: I should go.

MARSHA: Wait. (Handing back his dog tags.) These are yours.

JAMES: I'll hold onto them.

MARSHA: Let Kelly wear them. It means you'll come back for him. It means he'll wait for you.

JAMES: Yes. I will.

MARSHA: We have sixteen more years?

JAMES: At least.

MARSHA: Maybe more?

JAMES: Maybe.

MARSHA: I wish your father could see the man you've grown into.

JAMES: I wish he could see me, too.

MARSHA: I'm so glad I got to see you.

    (He takes two steps back, Stage Right)

JAMES: Can you? See me?

MARSHA: Yes.

    (He is slowly backing up.)

JAMES: Can you see me?

MARSHA: Yes.

(He is offstage.)

JAMES (off) Can you see me?

MARSHA: Yes, Jimmy! (Waving, excited) James! James!

(JIMMY runs on from Left.)

JIMMY: What?! I'm right here. (MARSHA turns.) Where you can see me.

(A moment frozen in time. MARSHA studies her son.)

JIMMY: What's wrong?

(MARSHA opens her arms. JIMMY runs to her. MARSHA embraces her son.)

BLACKOUT.

END OF PLAY.

LOVE SONG

Poem by Melody Wilson

For hundreds of years, mothers in the Indian village of Kongthong have named newborns with individual melodies. Each song lasts 15 or 20 seconds and remains with the child for life.

—Atlas Obscura, "The Indian Village Where Every Person's Name is a Unique Song"

Afternoon must be a perpetual
canon of rise and fall
with every child a song.
Greetings linger as children gallop
playground to porch, remove shoes,
wash faces. Even the surly
endure the contours
of their mothers' love
all the way through,
no cutting her off in the middle
with an exasperated cluck.
The song flows to a conclusion
they already know. Time rides the
current of sound, beginning to end,
slows them down, settles them
for dinner, for bed,
serenades them
all the way home.

THE SHADOW OF A DECISION

Fiction by Susan Field

I opened the back door of my grandmother's house and entered the kitchen. The smell of bread dough rising set my stomach to grumble. I lingered and imagined eating the whole loaf with thick slabs of butter. That wouldn't happen because there was little to spare. Bread, milk from our cow Babe, last summer's canned spinach, and a few eggs were all Grandmother, two uncles, two aunts, and I had for our suppers. It seemed even the chickens were hungry and less productive that winter of 1933 during the hard times.

My uncle Ernst, who called me by my nickname, asked, "How's our little Robin?"

I hesitated before answering. Usually when I came home from school, Grandmother was busy washing in the stand-alone zinc sink, cooking, or mending clothes. Ernst spent his days looking for work, any job that would help us afford to stay in our house. That day Grandmother and Ernst sat at the table, which was uncommon and troublesome. Grandmother, who wore a yellow apron over her housedress, clutched a letter in her coarse hands. Ernst, in blue coveralls, held an opened white envelope. The tea kettle, one of Grandmother's few luxuries, clattered an aggravating hiss on the wood stove as it heated water.

Her constant reprimand, "Idle hands are sinful hands," came to mind. The two of them sitting in the middle of the afternoon looked like idle hands, like sinning. Or trouble. I worried we had to move again, or maybe someone was hurt. Or worse yet, dead.

My footsteps into the room were slow and slight. I answered Ernst's question. "Today I learned how to divide numbers."

Grandmother, whose face held wrinkles like a newly plowed wheat field, waved her arm and barked an order to me. "Eleanor, get along. Do your chores." I tiptoed toward the bedroom, but dawdled and listened by the doorsill.

"One thing's for sure," Ernst said, his voice wavering. "If he's coming in two weeks to get her, we need to protect her." Uncle Ernst was like that—he often looked out for me.

"What you getting at?" asked Grandmother. Feeding all of us, taking care of the farm animals, clothing us, and getting us to church left little for her to give affection. And I sensed weariness in her voice.

I pressed one ear hard to the wall to hear better. Ernst spoke with tight, staccato words. "Look. It's not good. I don't want her hurt. We got to warn her. If he wants her, and you write back and say no, we'll have to watch out for him." The chair creaked as if he shifted his weight. "Haydon's a scoundrel. He might try to steal her away. That's what I'm talking about." He started whispering, and I had to strain to hear. "And, you remember what he did to our dear Margarete."

"Quiet." Grandmother's remark had a decided snap to it.

Haydon? Margarete? They were talking about my father and mother. I pulled my coat tighter around me, every part of my body stiffened, except my right foot started thumping nervously. I peeked around the corner.

"Haydon's not fit to take care of her." Grandmother said, hissing like her tea kettle and shaking the letter until it rustled.

"Well, he's got the law on his side," said Ernst.

They sat unmoving. In the hall with shadows of heavy greens and grays, sour heat flipped in my stomach as I ducked out of sight.

When I was younger, Grandmother told me Father couldn't take care of me after my mother died in a car accident. That was why I lived with her and her children. But one day when she didn't think I could hear, she told Ernst, "Haydon's a drunken bootlegger. He was a no-good to Margarete and hit her."

Grandmother's shoes scraped the kitchen floor. She sighed, got up, and plodded toward the cookstove. "My dear Margarete…" Her sad voice trailed off.

Six weeks after my father's letter and Grandmother's refusal to send me back to him, she received a court order. She told me, "We have to travel to Washington and see a judge in the Snohomish County Court."

I didn't know what a court was. The way she said it, with worry in her voice, sounded bad.

Grandmother and I arrived at the depot in Pendleton on the next Sunday. The train engine with its tall stack belched thick smoke, clouding the air with a hot, sooty smell. Amid the banging of passengers dragging trunks on the platform and the conductor calling out, Grandmother's orders bellowed. "Eleanor. Follow me inside. We have to buy our tickets." Minutes later, we boarded the Pacific Mountain Railroad train.

She squeezed my hand and pulled me down the aisle to a wooden seat. "Get settled. It's a long ride that'll take all day." The train lurched forward with metal-on-metal screeching. I pressed my hands to my ears as the great whistle pierced the morning air.

I grew tired of traveling after a while and asked her, "Will my father be there? What's going to happen? What's a judge?"

Grandmother blew out a sigh, pinched the bridge of her nose between her thumb and first finger like she did when she was worried. "I'll be there."

It occurred to me that maybe Grandmother didn't know what would happen either. What had she told me several times? "Just remember. When the judge asks who you want to live with, don't say your father. You'd be making a big mistake."

I then settled and played with my rag doll, Little Mary. Over time, I had loved her up so much her cloth arms dangled from single threads and her sewn-in blue eyes frayed. In that quiet moment, a baby across the aisle suckled under a blanket. The mother hummed a sweet tune to the baby while its smacking lips gulped her milk. When the baby cooed, she shared the tender moment with her husband.

"Look John, he's smiling at you." The man turned and gazed at the young'un. A girl, about the same age as I was, slept with her head on the man's lap. Once when I peeked over, the father stroked the girl's curly hair. His hands were clean, unlike my uncles' whose fingernails were filled with grime from the chicken coop, Babe, or grease from their tinkering.

I stared out the window and was startled when Grandmother jerked and snorted in her sleep. In her lap lay the Holy Bible, open to a passage. Instead of a strict grandmother, I longed for a mother's pleasing voice to sing to me and a loving father to pat my hair. I touched my head and fantasized about Mother caressing away my worries. However, all I felt was my straight, brown, braided hair.

Soon, the rhythmic clack, clack of the train calmed me and I dozed. When I woke, the peter-pan collar of my moss green dress was soaked because I had a fearsome nightmare that Grandmother left me alone by a road. From that point forward, I sat still. I didn't want to upset her on whose good graces I relied, and who took that long trip because of me, even though she couldn't afford it.

We rolled into Seattle. I stepped off the train, and my insides somersaulted. This would be the first time since I was a baby to see my father. I didn't remember how he talked, how he moved, or smelled. Grandmother and I walked into the station lobby where whiffs of sweat, scuffed leather, and dust drifted among the travelers who crisscrossed the sizeable room. Announcements over a loud speaker pierced in a jumble of noises so loud it hurt my ears.

"Haydon's going to meet us. I don't like it, but he's got a car. He's taking us to a boarding house." Grandmother scanned the area and said, "There he is." She pointed to a man with a pudgy face whose gut hung over his belt. He stood at the refreshment counter, leaning toward a young lady. He tilted his head back, opened his mouth, and laughed above the noisy racket.

I heard what he sounded like, and he was loud. We headed toward him; Grandmother's sturdy shoes clomped on the stone floor.

"Haydon." Her sharp tone warned me she was tired from the long trip.

He turned toward us. I stood stiffly as I watched the barrel-shaped man in a striped suit with broad shoulders approach. On his head was a gray Fedora hat. When he bent down to greet me, I jerked away. His head loomed large—bigger than Grandmother's enamel dishpan—and his breath stunk.

"Well, well. Aren't you a scrawny thing?" He chuckled and tousled my hair with his thick hand. I didn't like strangers touching me. I thought of the father who affectionately patted the girl's curls on the train; my father was nothing like him. I shrank away from him and my knees wobbled.

From the station lobby, we walked outside to Father's big black sedan. Lights on the outsides of the building shone enough I could see my reflection in the car's polished fender. He opened the door, and I climbed onto the back seat. Grandmother sat in the front. The cool, soft leather felt like butter tasted—smooth and creamy; and plush fabric lined the inside roof. I fingered the slick metal around the window and tried to avoid smearing it with my grimy hands.

When we reached the boardinghouse, Father lifted me out of the car. I squirmed and tried to wiggle out of his clutch. At the door, he told me, "I'll see ya at ten so I can show you the town."

Grandmother's head whipped around, and her angry eyes glared straight at him. "She's staying here with me!"

Haydon spread his shoulders and met her refusal with a rough laugh. I glanced from Grandmother's stern face and folded arms to Father's smirk.

"Uh hum." He cleared his throat. "I *am* her father."

Grandmother's lips squeezed into a scowl, and she shut the door as Father stomped his foot down on the threshold. "She'll stay with me until the court date."

"You forget. She's mine. I'm picking her up tomorrow."

"You don't remember. After Margarete died, you said you didn't want your own child. So, I've had her. You'll see her in two days."

His snort mocked, boomed as he turned, and walked away. "Tomorrow!"

The boarding house walls shook when Grandmother slammed the front door.

The next morning, Father announced to Grandmother, "I'm here."

Her face flattened. A rush of red marbled up her neck and neither spoke.

Father broke the silence. "I'll be takin' good care of her."

Grandmother's jaw tightened as she leaned her body forward and squinted straight into his face. She and Father looked like two dogs ready to fight. "Be back by noon." Her words sizzled. "Eleanor, get your coat on." She bent down and whispered in my ear. "Mind yourself and be careful around him."

Father and I left. My arm, shaking from fear, waved a weak goodbye. Once I settled on the front seat, I slid my body as far from him as I could. The engine revved.

"Did ya' know I'm a salesman? But I make most o' my money playing poker…er, I mean playing games and selling spirits."

Spirits. Finally, something I recognized. I knew about the Holy Spirit from church members who received the divine touch. I was surprised Father had The Spirit in him. He must be a God-fearing man. Holy and church-going. Although, I couldn't figure out how a man could play games and earn money because Grandmother never allowed playing games in the house. To her, they were sinful. I thought he must have special games.

Soon, Father said, "I know you don't know me real good, but I'm your daddy. Your old granny, she don't love you. Why, look at what you're wearing."

I looked down at myself, embarrassed at my dingy dress, floppy hand-me-down shoes that were too big for my short feet, and socks with holes in the heels.

"I can buy you lots o' new clothes. You're my daughter, and I want you livin' with me. I'd treat you real special. See, I'm gonna run for Sheriff and one o' my buddies said if I wanna get elected, I need to show I'm a family man."

We soon parked in front of a tall building. Father said, "This is the fanciest shop in town. Just like I promised."

We climbed a wide staircase until we reached the second floor. Father found three dresses and a gray coat with a black velvet collar. In the shoe section, I hid my feet as I pulled off my scruffy shoes and exposed my holey socks. I slipped on a pair of Mary Janes and they fit. Best of all, they were brand new. With my toes to the floor, I pivoted my foot from right to left, admiring the patent leather and thick soles.

"Those look good. I'll take 'em," he said to the clerk. His money clip bulged with bills, and he pointed. "The toys is over there. Go have a look around."

Toys! My head nearly spun while I scanned the area. I had never seen so many toys. I skipped a few steps with delight, then slowed and began to search. Here were dolls, brown teddy bears, boxes of trains, puzzles, wooden doll houses with delicate furniture, balls, tops, and play cars. The packed shelves thrilled me. In the excitement, one item caught my attention. I stopped in the middle of the aisle and stared up at a pink box high on a ledge with a pretty doll inside. I looked to Father, ready to ask him for help to get the doll down, but he was talking and laughing with a saleslady at the counter.

A passing clerk found me admiring the doll. "Her name is Madeline. She's a real cutie, isn't she? Would you like me to show you?"

I nodded, wide-eyed. The salesgirl reached to the top shelf and lifted the box down into my open arms. I fell in love instantly.

Madeline. Her face with delicate features matched the musical sound of her name. She was the most beautiful dolly I'd ever seen. I stared at Madeline through the cellophane window on the box. I twirled. My braids flew as if they sang a duet in tandem. My heart thumped while I looked at the doll's bright blue eyes. They blinked! Really blinked. Madeline's light brown hair curled around her soft, painted pink cheeks. I hugged the box and wanted to tear off the cardboard, pull Madeline out of the package, and cuddle her. I imagined playing house with the sweet doll, taking her to my favorite tree in the afternoons, and singing to her at night.

Father paid for her as I squeezed the box with Madeline and my dreams inside.

On the ride back, Father asked, "That was fun, wasn't it? You can have all them things. They're what you always wanted, ain't they?"

I thought about them. A wool coat with a soft collar. A pair of shoes—the first that didn't have holes in the soles stuffed with cardboard to protect my feet from the snow and rain. Three dresses, one frilly with lace. A new doll.

Maybe he wasn't a bogeyman like Grandmother and Ernst said. My mind circled. I finally uttered, "I love my dolly."

"Good. You can have her and all the rest of the stuff." Father's voice softened like a sweet song. "If you want these, you can keep 'em. You just gotta tell the judge you're gonna live with me. If you tell the judge you want to go back to your granny's rat hole, I'll take 'em and give 'em to some other girl." He eyed me. "Understand?"

I didn't understand. His words no longer like a song anymore. They sounded like a trick and resembled a mad dog's threatening growl. I stayed quiet.

Before returning me to Grandmother, Father stopped at his house and carried the packages inside. "Bring that doll."

I trudged up the front steps. At the top, I clung to the box with Madeline, rocked it in my arms, and kissed the clear covering. My father snatched it out of my arms, and I turned my head away.

Father's words, "They'll be here tomorrow when ya' come home with me," didn't reassure me. My insides churned because his promise didn't feel genuine.

Tuesday morning meant Grandmother and I had to go to court. I picked at my breakfast. The thick mush lumped in my throat.

"Finish up," said Grandmother, "we need to leave."

We soon walked to the courthouse. March gusts, blowing in from the Sound, slanted the winter's rain into our faces. Amid the briny air and fish tang, white sea birds screeched as they flew one direction, stopped in mid-flight, and darted another direction in the chaotic winds. Grandmother clutched my hand. My fingers ached, and I tried to loosen her grip. Instead, she held my hand even closer to her body. As we entered a massive building, I couldn't tell if she was mad or if she was scared, too.

I wiped rain away from my face as we hurried down a long hall. We took a seat on an empty wooden bench. Father stood on the other side of the room. He smiled at me, winked, and watched me sit down. I lowered my eyes and then stared straight ahead. Dark wood paneled the walls. Two flags on poles hung on each side of the judge's bench. I waited and grew impatient until the judge strode in with his black robe. We had to rise and sit down again. That time I tucked my hands under my thighs and willed them to stop shaking.

Although the judge said words I couldn't figure out, I understood one thing. I had to tell him who I wanted to live with. Grandmother. Or Father. I gulped hard when the judge commanded me to walk forward to his bench. My footsteps on the hard wood floor echoed. I shivered so much my teeth chattered. When the judge, sitting high above me, asked me who I wanted to live with, my mind swirled like a summer's dust devil. Although Father scared me, I wondered, did he love me? Did he really want me? Could I have a good life with him? And maybe a mother?

I thought more. Why did Grandmother warn me to stay away?

I knew children were supposed to obey their parents, and at church I recited the Ten Commandments, "Honor thy father and thy mother." I no longer had my mother, and I didn't know Father. My mind swayed back and forth between two worlds. My current life with strict grandmother, my aunts and uncles in the old, leaking shack was familiar. There were even a few good times. The summer before when we climbed the grassy slopes of the Blue Mountains to pick wild lupines and buttercups, and when we sang hymns together in the evenings.

I peered up at the judge's face. I had to reveal my private feelings to a stranger and make a decision that I didn't think any of my eight-year-old friends ever had to answer. The silence in the room throbbed in my knees.

Time stopped.

I looked at the judge, then glanced at Grandmother. I turned my head and found Father's face as he perched on the edge of the seat. I then focused back on the judge, inhaled and blurted. "I want to live with my grandmother."

The gavel pounded. It banged so loudly I barely heard the judge say, "Mrs. Delores Bowerman will now serve as the legal guardian of Eleanor Owens."

Grandmother blew out a sigh of relief. She came from behind and gave me a brief hug. Father stomped out of the room. His heels struck the floor, rumbling like thunder. Grandmother took my arm, and we left.

Father didn't even say goodbye. Tears almost squeezed out of my eyes, but what good was crying? No Mother. No Father. My shoulders slumped under the weight of his stinging anger.

Traveling home on the train, I wanted to shove the visit, the courtroom scene into the back of my mind and never think about them again. Try as I might, I couldn't. The shadow of the decision darkened my thinking. So, I gripped my rag doll, Little Mary. She wasn't Madeline, but she was more precious to me than the frilly dresses. More loving than my own Father. I adored her and would never trick her to love me.

DREAM AS GYPSY MOTH

Poem by Ace Englehart

   1. Shenandoah, 1991: GYPSY MOTHS CHANGE FACE OF NATIONAL PARK
          For no particular reason at this point in either of their lives, a
        particular man and a particular woman met at a party when
the gypsy moth larvae struck with a vengeance in
the shenandoah valley that summer
                        married when she met him, both
              divorced now, here—ponytail a little longer, singing
            to her a little louder—and that's all it takes
          to hold the hand of a man and believe
              in the sounds of change.
                Still, on a quiet May morning
            when the rain taps the tent just so,
*   the defoliated canopy alters the microclimate—and she burns*
within—overeating the host

   2.
Our first family outing:
the only thing you remember / there on
the canal: a little pink sock, rushed through
   a puddle on the way in / down by the
river, every eye wide while walking down the
aisle,
   up into the canopy he promised you—
some stars, the moon, and all of ESPN
Sportscenter (at forty-percent off no less), he's
the cameraman—
   your appetite controlled / you will not return
home: your oldest daughter will carry fire,

and this one—the yet unnamed,
unkown you carry inside:
*the female's ability to fly and defoliate, if repeated,
can lead to the death of forests*—she will be a forest.

3. October, 1991.

4. a dream, suspended
*lost in dreams / drawn to flames like the
deep in voices—fathers who left, lovers who
promised not but did—each a cold dark pocket
of ocean, and then / this body / within my body
/ is that world-holding, tip-toe-across-a-cold-
kitchen-floor-dancing / always a flame—
moonlight, fridge-light, campfire-don't-need-a-
flashlight—never a fire.*

I do not blame
the moth for the loss of
her life—I will learn to ask for more.

ARTESIA, NEW MEXICO

Nonfiction by Celia Ruiz

Artesia, New Mexico, was small and monotonous but the terrain was alive with spirits. By high noon the merciless sun bleached the sky white, and a lethargic stillness enveloped the town. Even scorpions and lizards dared not venture out. The silence was punctuated only by the occasional swish of dust devils that listlessly chased sagebrush balls. At dusk, fire-red skies loomed over the dark purple mesas and plateaus, and pink clouds shifted across the horizon. Men wore cowboy boots to stomp rattlers. And women stayed home. They would languidly fan their faces as sweat mixed with the ubiquitous red dust, leaving red streaks like the war paint of the Comanche or Apache.

Neighbors would drop in unannounced to chat or have coffee. Doors were left unlocked and children freely roamed the hills and streets. No one left Artesia, and no one moved in. But we were prepared. Our school was built underground, a cement fallout shelter. And of course we were always on the lookout for silver orbs in the skies, in case the Roswell aliens returned.

There were no yards or sidewalks. Homes were either crumbling adobe or rotting wood, with plywood covering broken windows and black tar paper patching holes in roofs. We lived literally on the wrong side of the railroad tracks, in a two-room adobe, its gaping holes exposing errant threads of straw. Every morning, I would wet and sweep our dirt floor to keep it hard. We had a rickety outhouse that sat in the distance, malodorous and dank. Food was scarce, and our staple was *atole*: ground corn and water.

My baby brother and I had been abandoned by our mother when she ran off with her lover while our father fought a war in Korea. We lived with our paternal grandmother, Tilana, waiting for our father to return and claim us.

We slept on the dirt floor, next to a metal twin bed that my fourteen-year-old aunt Petra slept on. My baby brother was named Alejandro

Junior, so I called him Papi to distinguish him from my father, Alejandro, who was Papa. We had not seen our mother in almost three years, and I had forgotten her face, her name, her smell, her voice.

My grandmother Tilana told me that my mother had run off with a man named Beto, whom she had met at the Gomez Club in Hagerman, New Mexico, just outside Carlsbad. Tilana would tell me that my mother loved Beto more than she loved my father, and for that matter more than she loved me and my brother.

Maybe my grandmother was right. After all, my mother did leave me at some stranger's home. Just me and the clothes I was wearing. She told me to try to be good and that she would be back. At first I thought she had only thrown me away and kept my baby brother, Papi, but I later learned that she had abandoned him as well, at some other distant relative's house. We probably would still be at these strangers' homes, had our father not been given special privilege to leave the Korean War and return to gather us up and divorce our mother. You see, Papa had privileges most regular soldiers didn't have because he was a highly decorated World War II hero.

I remember the night he returned to pick me up. I was asleep on the sofa when I felt a tickle in my stomach. I jerked upright, thinking something bad was happening. As my vision focused, I saw my father, his eyes bright and happy, kissing me and calling me his *güera fea*, or his ugly fair-skinned one, his joking term of endearment for me that really meant "my beautiful fair one."

When I saw him, instead of feeling relief, I was overwhelmed with anger. I kicked, yelled, and pushed him away. He laughed even harder, and held me close until I exhausted myself, whimpered and clung to him, afraid that he would disappear or, worse, that I would wake up and it would all have been a vicious nightmare.

During his visit, Papa stayed with us at Tilana's house for several weeks. He was not the same happy, gregarious person he had been when we lived together at Fort Bliss. He no longer threw me in the air, laughing, tickling me, and kissing my face. He sat smoking cigarettes and staring absently into space. Once I saw him with red eyes, tears streaming down his cheeks. Tilana told me that he had almost killed himself when he got the letter telling him Mother had run off with another man. He put his gun to his head and would have pulled the trigger had a soldier in his unit not jumped up and stopped him.

My father could not stay with us. He had to return to fight the war in Korea. He promised that he would return for me. But the days turned to weeks, weeks turned to months, and months to years. And I waited.

When I arrived in Artesia, I was a plump three-and-a-half year old, but within a year, I was a skinny, bowed-legged little girl, with unruly wavy hair and a faraway look in my eye. I recognize that look in photos I see of Anne Frank, staring beyond the pain.

I would go to bed with my stomach growling. One night I had a vivid dream of rows upon rows of chocolate candies and cookies in front of me. I could smell the chocolate, vanilla, butter, and caramelized sugar. The dream was so real that I stretched out my arms, snatching as many goodies as I could. I woke up to find my skinny arms flailing in the dark, grabbing the cold air.

The house was quiet. The silvery beams of the full moon shone through the thick adobe window sills, casting shadows in the room. A deep thirst overcame me.

I walked toward the kitchen and saw a glass of white liquid next to the faucet. *Milk!* I ran and gulped down the grainy liquid. Within seconds a burning sensation filled my esophagus. My stomach began to convulse. Hot projectiles of bile and vomit spewed from my mouth. I was writhing on the ground covered in my vomit when my grandmother came out, furious that I had woken up everyone.

What I had thought was milk had been Tide soap mixed with water that my grandmother used to wash dishes.

To this day, I hate milk.

My grandmother Tilana was a force to be reckoned with—intense, demanding, and possessed. I both respected and feared her. She had strong Indigenous features, with long black hair, high cheekbones, deep-set, steely almond-shaped eyes, and skin that looked like old, creased buckskin. She was loving and attentive at times, but when she got angry, she was meaner than a rattlesnake. Her face would crinkle, her body puff, and she would let out piercing yelps. We knew she was on the warpath, and we would be wise to hide.

Some people whispered that she was a *curandera*, a healer. I don't know if she was or not, but I would see her go out into the desert at high noon to gather plants, cacti, scorpion larvae, rattlesnake tails, and bird feathers. I would watch as she took out strange-smelling ingredients and boiled them on the wood-burning stove, filling the house with the scents of oil, dirt, wind, leaves, and decay.

"*Abuelita*, what are you doing?" I asked once, when the bittersweet smell of the simmering herbs irritated my nose and throat.

"*Mija*," she answered in her husky voice, "I'm making a special medicine for Papi's stomachaches."

"That's not medicine. It's just grasses and junk!" I exclaimed.

She stopped stirring her pot. She stooped down to glare into my eyes and, in a low and serious whisper that was almost otherworldly, said, "Celia, there is so much you need to learn about. Do you want me to tell you a secret?"

I stood still and nodded yes.

"Listen to me carefully. Plants, trees, insects—all living things have spirit and healing power. One day I will teach you to listen to their voices and feel their energy."

"Plants don't talk!" I blurted.

Her eyes narrowed as she continued. "Plants will share their secrets if you listen. The trees, the plants will help us in times of need if we approach them and ask respectfully. My people have been working with plant medicine for generations, *mija*."

I opened my hand and showed her the handful of roly-poly bugs I carried around with me, my special friends. "Can insects talk? Can you teach me to talk to my bugs?"

A crack of a smile broke through. "Yes, some insects, animals, and birds carry messages. But not all bugs are open to sharing their secrets with us. Look at your bugs. See how they curl into a ball when you touch them? See how they harden into their shell, too afraid to look at you? Fear is keeping them caged. You have to open your heart to know the ways of the universe."

It was gobbledygook to me. She sometimes said and did the strangest things. I ran off with my bugs, taking them everywhere, talking to them, building them mud houses, even sneaking them to sleep with me on the floor hoping that one day they would talk to me.

For a while—after my uncle Tacho died in a cotton gin accident in Pecos, Texas—my great-grandmother Doña Selza came to live with us in Artesia. Doña Selza wore thick stockings, covered her head in a bandana, and created her own foul-smelling concoctions.

If Tilana was a force, her mother was a terrifying power of nature: stern, stocky, impatient, and explosive. Doña Selza would curse and raise her walking cane at us, thrashing it about, ready to break our bones. When I was bored, I would tiptoe behind her, yank her dress, and stick my tongue out at her, as she hopped, cursed, and violently swung at me.

Doña Selza came from the Rio Grande Valley, part of the band of pioneers who settled Fort Davis, Texas. They survived Comanche attacks, the Texas Rangers, and the unforgiving terrain of the Chihuahua high desert. They lived insular lives. Even today, many residents are still over ninety-five percent Indigenous, attesting to the isolated nature of the area.

One day, as I was digging and gathering bugs, I stepped over a rotting apple and a bee flew up into my dress. I jumped and screamed as it buzzed and stung me. Then I ran into the house, spilling a jar of fermenting herbs onto the dirt floor.

Tilana shook her head. Her black eyes receded into the deep folds of her face. She decided I had too much energy and that I needed exorcism. Whippings had not worked; dunking my head in a tub of cold, dirty water had not drowned my naughty spirit. She yanked me by the ear and pulled me to the wood-burning stove, where an effervescent black liquid gurgled.

She told me to take off all my clothes but for my T-shirt and underwear. She then pulled me to a chair in front of the stove and reached for a mesquite branch that she dipped in a bucket of water and herbs. She shook off the excess water and brushed my body with it. "Stay still," she then said as she moved a bowl with burning incense up and down in front of my body and chanted a prayer in a language that was neither English nor Spanish.

The smell of the incense was spicy and sweet like cinnamon. "Open your eyes," she said as she continued her incomprehensible chant.

"There," she said, smiling at me, "that should quell that frenetic energy of yours."

I felt a tingling sensation, as if some invisible energy source had washed over my body. I ran and looked at myself in the mirror. I was disappointed to see that I was still the same skinny, restless little girl as before.

That was the summer two strangers came and whisked me away from Artesia.

It was an unremarkable day. By noon, the sun reached its apex, scorching the red earth. Papi and I were foraging for sparkly treasures in the deep gorge behind our house. I tasted the rivulets of salty red sweat that streamed down my face as I made dust balls with a stick. A car slowly drove up and stopped a few feet away. It was a brand-new black car, with shimmering chrome around its headlights, bouncing off like a million diamonds.

A sullen, dark-skinned man with a thin mustache sat behind the steering wheel. Next to him was a beautiful and elegant woman with long black wavy hair, thick black eyelashes that framed her hazel eyes, and translucent white skin with a rosy blush on her high cheekbones. She slipped out of the car. She was wearing a beige suit with a tailored jacket that showed off her small waist, a mid-calf pencil skirt, black-seamed stockings, and a string of pearls.

I had never seen anyone so beautiful.

"*Celia, soy yo, tu mama*; I am your mother," the lovely lady said in two languages to make sure I understood, looking at me as if I were a crazed jackrabbit she had to entice.

Just then, Tilana rushed out of the house shrieking. I had never before noticed how old and shabby my grandmother looked in her loose-fitting cotton print dress, the faded apron stained with food and dirt tied tightly around her bulging stomach. Her body was upright, stiff, her fists clenched, and flames exploded in her eyes. She would get that same look when I had done something wrong, but this time her wrath was directed at the glamorous stranger.

"*¿Que quieres aqui, Licha?* You're not wanted here!" Tilana screamed.

My aunt Petra ran to me and whispered, "That's your mother, and she's here to take you and Papi to California."

"She's not my mother! I'm not going!" I yelled as I picked up a handful of rocks and dirt and threw them at the beautiful lady with the hazel eyes and ran into our crumbling house looking for a place to hide. No one had told me anything about a mother coming for me. I grabbed a metal hairbrush that was on the kitchen counter and hid in my secret corner, a partially collapsed wall at the back of the house. I rolled into a tight ball, held my breath, and gripped the hairbrush as I waited.

I could hear Tilana's high-pitched voice, filled with rancor and despair. "You can't take them, Licha! You threw them away! You just want the child support money from the army. Leave them here!"

"Get out of the way, old lady, you can't stop me," the lady screeched back. "*Vieja mendiga.* Look at how dirty and skinny they are, their heads full of lice, *piojos*. You can't take good care of them. Alejandro told me I could take them with me to California!" I was startled to hear anyone yell back at my grandmother. And I thought it must be a lie—my father would never give us away like that. He told me he was coming back for me. Why didn't Tilana use her mystical powers and make this woman disappear?

I closed my eyes tightly, held my breath, and tried to invoke one of my grandmother's chants as I repeated to myself, *They will not find me if I stay quiet and don't move. I will make myself invisible.*

Between my silent chanting and the sound of my heart battering in my ears, I did not hear the steps coming toward my corner. The arm of the dark-skinned man with the thin mustache reached and pulled me from my hiding place. I kicked, bit, yelled, jerked my body up and down, twisted sideways, and threw the hairbrush at him. He overpowered me, held me like a sack of potatoes, and lugged me to the waiting car as I hollered and kicked.

The lady who said she was my mother laughed and said, "She's a handful, that Celia. Just like her Aunt Lucia!"

"You're not my mother. I'm not leaving. My father is coming for me soon!" I yelled as I pounded my fists, bit, scratched, spit, anything to make this stop.

The man threw me in the back seat of the car, next to Papi, who was standing upright, frozen, his eyes wide and red. His face was streaked with dirt and he seemed to be turning purple as he held his breath.

The car started. Tilana ran after us, pulling at her long black wispy hair, cursing and letting out the most forlorn wail I had ever heard.

"Speed up," the lady told the man, "before that crazy *bruja* throws herself at our new car and scratches it."

As the car drove away, I turned back and saw Tilana, dropped to her knees, red dust swirling around her, her howls echoing off the distant hills—the same hills where she would walk for hours to collect her herbs and specimens.

Papi began to tremble and sob.

The lady lit a cigarette and turned on the radio. Happy Mexican accordion music drowned out my brother's sobs until he went catatonic. He refused to sit down, his eyes glazed over with terror. I placed my head on my knees and wrapped my arms around my legs, as my mind whirred with plans of how I would escape. After a few minutes, a stench of rotten eggs mixed with the smell of cigarettes. I looked up and saw

Papi's swollen tear-streaked face as he held his crotch; his pants were wet with a huge sagging load.

I placed my head back on my knees and closed my eyes, shutting out the scene, the smell of waste, urine, cigarette smoke, and perfume. My thoughts whirled. I would find my way back home to Artesia. I would run away once the car stopped. I wanted to go back to Fort Bliss. I wanted my father. I wanted to dissolve and disappear.

The memory of the rest of that trip is buried in the black hole where trauma and nightmares sleep.

ELEGY FOR MY FATHER

Poem by Dale Champlin

   I think by now you must have forgotten our trip.
As I remember it, we crossed the Atlantic.

   That morning you promised to swim only to the buoy.
I was the solid thirty-pounder gripping your throat

like a life saver. Around us sunlight spun waves

   into a gossamer net. Gulls screamed and soared
   as they flew inland making harsh V's with their wings.
I knew I was in way over my head, yours too.

   You were swimming the Australian crawl, fighting
into the current. I was clinging like a lamprey.

   It took us all morning to reach the Atlantic shelf.
Below us the continental slope deepened.

   Remember how schools of tuna flowed like traffic
beneath us, their bright glints rising to the surface?

   As saltwater dragged over your shoulders, you must
have become tired. I grew heavier after that.

   Behind us the coastline vanished and under us
the abyssal plain plunged obscure and foreboding.

   All day you swam while I dozed off and on, my fingers
clenched together. You relaxed into the breaststroke.

Resting my ear between your shoulder blades I could hear
your invisible heartbeat. That was when I started to ask,

How far do we still have to go? Night settled in,
its thick darkness rising into vast turbulence—

a cosmic ocean more immense than the one below.
Perhaps it's too late for you to remember

that you slept. I confess, a small child could not keep
her grip. I thought about how dead the water plunged.

I saw mountains crest deep below us. I can tell you now
all that I remember, to record it in your log.

Now I record it in mine. When the time came, we drifted.
    I don't know where you went, or if you reached

the opposite shore, but I continued my journey.
    I know that I survived without dreaming of you.

CONTRIBUTORS

JAN BAROSS's career began with painting, then documentary filmmaking and photography. Her film *Pioneer Women* premiered on A&E Channel. She taught filmmaking at Oregon State. She wrote award winning plays and screenplays and worked as a newspaper film critic. *Jose Builds a Woman*, her first novel, garnered first place for fiction in the Kay Snow Awards. It was blurbed by Ursula Le Guin. She was librettist for an opera based on her play, *Mata Hari*, that opened in Dallas, Texas. She has finished her new novel/fictional memoir, *Bye-Bye Bakersfield*. Find her at: janbaross.com.

KRISTIN BORK is a lifelong Oregonian who took a few detours after high school before landing back in Portland. She tries to make sense out of things by writing about them.

DALE CHAMPLIN is an Oregon poet with an MFA in fine art. Dale has poems published in *Willawaw, The Opiate, Visions International, San Pedro River Review, catheXis, Pif,* and elsewhere. She is the editor of */pān| dé| mik/ 2020: An Anthology of Pandemic Poems* from the Oregon Poetry Association. Her first collection, *The Barbie Diaries*, was published in 2019 with Just a Lark Books. Three collections, *Isadora, Callie Comes of Age,* and *Andromina, A Stranger in America* are forthcoming. Her sentient android, Andromina, protagonist of ninety-four poems, declares, "I wax magnetic as chunky biker jewelry, yet I'm susceptible to innuendo."

 **JEN CURRIN** has published five books, including the 2011 Audre Lorde Award-winning *The Inquisition Yours*, and the 2018 Globe and Mail Best Book *Hider/Seeker: Stories*. They live on the traditional, unceded, and ancestral territories of the Qayqayt, Musqueam, and Kwantlen First Nations in New Westminster, BC, Canada (a suburb of Vancouver).

 After a lifetime of teaching adolescents, **SUSAN DONNELLY** rediscovered herself and writing. She aims to create poems that are like old-fashioned keyholes, small openings that reveal larger worlds. She lives in Portland, Oregon, with her husband and newly adopted yearling labradoodle.

 **CIEL DOWNING**'s Blackfeet name is Motai Auksi Piksi Ahki: a writer who has lived in eight states and two countries, but found home in the woods by the Pacific Ocean. With a resume that includes dog track usher, park ranger, rancher, counseling psychologist, and veteran, she culls the words born of those experiences and encounters and tries to infuse them with the compassion, angst, resilience and gratitude these events have taught.

ACE ENGLEHART (previously published as Alexandra) is a Richmond, Virginia, native and recent MFA graduate in Poetry from the University of Tennessee, Knoxville with a BA in English from Virginia Commonwealth University. Her work has been featured in online magazines *Unlimited Literature, Persephone's Daughters, A Murder of Storytellers,* and VCU's *Poictesme (pwa-tem)*. Her recent thesis project, *This Body Divine,* is an interrogation of postcolonial "queer fear" and the consequential restraints placed on the LGBTQ+ community to suggest a future that embraces change rather than erases it. Outside of her poetic work, Ace enjoys photography, karaoke, camping and swimming, as well as spending time at home with her partner Holly and their three pets.

SUSAN K. FIELD lives in the Pacific Northwest and is a Willamette Writers member. She savors long walks in verdant forests, robins' spring songs, and fragrant lilies in her summer garden. Her published works include fiction, nonfiction and poetry.

ROBIN GOLDFIN is playwright, performer and teacher. He has produced work at Theater for the New City, The Midtown International Theater Festival, Artistic New Directions, and Stage Left Studios in New York. Other writing published in *Tikkun, Zeek,* and *The Gay and Lesbian Review Worldwide*; and in the anthologies *Queer Stories for Boys: True Stories from the Gay Men's Storytelling*

Workshop and *One on One: The Best Men's Monologues for the 21st Century*. Last project: *Suddenly, a Knock at the Door*, a play based on stories by Etgar Keret, with music by Oren Neiman, and directed by David Carson. "Kelly Green" was first produced in the Eclectic Evening of Shorts with the ANDTheatre Company in New York in 2020.

GABRIEL MATTHEW GRANILLO is a graduate of Northern Arizona University with a BS in Journalism. His fiction and poetry have been published in both print and online journals including *Vortex, Postcard Poems and Prose*, and *Flash Fiction Magazine*. He is a writer, journalist, and photographer living in Portland, Oregon.

KATE GRAY's latest poetry collection, *For Every Girl: New & Selected Poems* (Widow & Orphan House, 2019) presents a chronicle of queer affirmation. Her first novel, *Carry the Sky*, (Forest Avenue, 2014) stares at bullying without blinking. Her book of poems, *Another Sunset We Survive* (2007) was a finalist for the Oregon Book Award and followed chapbooks, *Bone-Knowing* (2006, Gertrude Press Poetry Prize), and *Where She Goes* (2000, Blue Light Chapbook Prize). She's been awarded residencies at Hedgebrook, Norcroft, and Soapstone, and a fellowship from Oregon Literary Arts. She lives with her partner and an impetuous dog in Mosier, Oregon.

MICHAEL HANNER is an architect whose poems are found in *Timberline Review, Nimrod, Cloudbank, Rhino, Southern Humanities Review, Gargoyle, Mudfish* and others. His most recent books are *Avenida Uriburu*, 2014, *October*, 2015 and *Adriatica*, 2016 and a guide book, *Le Bugue, Black Périgord & Beyond*, 2016. He loves Toni Hanner, sharp scissors, Esterbrook pens, travel, irony, English croquet, French cooking, Argentine tango, and photography.

SUZY HARRIS lives in Portland, Oregon. Her poems have appeared most recently in *Clackamas Literary Review, Williwaw*, and *Rain* and are forthcoming in *Switchgrass Review*.

MARIE HARTUNG writes from her living room recliner in the small-ish town of Monroe, WA. She earned two MFA's in the Whidbey Island Writers' Workshop and has a day job as a Realtor. Her work has appeared in *Slab, Talking River, Thin Air, Third Wednesday, WA 129, Clackamas Review, Crosswinds Review*, plus several anthologies. Annually, she is a judge for National Bisexual Book Awards. She has two sons age 15 and 17 who are the love of her life, although, NY pizza is a close second. She is working on finding a publisher for her full-length memoir.

ASHLEY HAY is a recent college graduate, occasional freelance content creator, enthusiastic bookseller, and lifelong writer based in Corvallis, Oregon. She dabbles in writing of all forms, but has a particular love for poetry and short stories. She has been published in *Bluefire Journal*, Oregon State University's *Prism*, and various blogs across the Internet. One day, she aspires to eventually study rhetoric in graduate school and own at least three cats.

LAURA HERBST has just completed her first novel. Set in Togo, West Africa, where she served as a Peace Corps volunteer and a Fulbright fellow, the novel tells the story of Casey Combs, 24, a Ph.D. researcher who returns to Togo, West Africa, with the sacred power objects which her Evangelist uncle stole. She is honored to have received the Doris Betts Fiction Prize. Her work has been published in *The Sun, The Tishman Review, North Carolina Literary Review, Confrontation*, and is upcoming in *F(r)iction*.

BILLIE HUDSON is a queer writer, professor, parent, and commuter. She writes books and publishes in magazines, newspapers, and peer-reviewed academic journals.

MALLORY KELLUM is a French-American student studying at Corban University. She is a seeker of finding beauty in the in-betweens and spends her spare time learning from new friends from across the world. When she's not enjoying moldy cheese and French wine, she writes, inspired by the freedom found in living life with God.

RUTH Q. LEIBOWITZ lives in Portland, Oregon, with a warm purring creature. She has had work published in *Hippocampus, Soul-Lit, Five on the Fifth, As You Were, Peregrine*, and *Calyx*. She is grateful to her writing community for their existence and support.

HAYLEY MCCOY is a writer who lives in Corvallis, Oregon. She loves rainy day bookshops, tromping to the river with her kids, and stories that take her away. She's also fond of rain boots, friendly chickens, and sunshine. She is currently working on a novel.

AMY MILLER's poetry and nonfiction have appeared in *Barrow Street, Copper Nickel, Gulf Coast, Tupelo Quarterly, Willow Springs*, and *ZYZZYVA*. Her full-length poetry collection *The Trouble with New England Girls* won the Louis Award from Concrete Wolf Press, and her chapbooks include *I Am on a River and Cannot Answer* (BOAAT Press) and *Rough House* (White Knuckle Press). She lives in Ashland, Oregon. writers-island.blogspot.com.

SARAH MOTT a four-year veteran of the Girl Scouts and writes speculative fiction, mostly science fiction. In "real life," she sells machined metal components to commercial Spacecraft manufacturers and dreams of humankind one day colonizing other worlds. Before this career, she was a West Point graduate and a combat veteran in the Middle East.

TOBIAS PETERSON's work has appeared in *Lunch Ticket, Superstition Review, Ghost City Press, Coldnoon*, and elsewhere. He holds an MFA in Poetry from Texas State University and has taught writing in Texas, England, Spain, and most recently at Clark College in Vancouver, Washington. He lives across the Columbia River from there, in Portland, Oregon. Visit him at tobiaspeterson.com.

CELIA M RUIZ is a retired employment lawyer living in Portland, Oregon. "Artesia, New Mexico," is part of her larger memoir, "My Name is Not Sally," which is about her trajectory from a high school dropout and welfare mother to a University of California, Berkeley Law School graduate. It explores the assault on the human spirit of pervasive poverty and discrimination against Mexican Americans. Ms. Ruiz was a finalist in the journal *Don't Talk to Me About Love*, 2017 Prose Contest which published her piece, "The Visit." Ms. Ruiz is active with writing groups in the Portland, Oregon, and San Francisco Bay area.

STEPHANIE STRIFFLER has loved and written poetry almost all her life. She recently retired after decades of public service as a lawyer for the people of Oregon. Her poems have appeared in publications including *Calyx*, *Voicecatcher*, *Timberline Review*, and *Persimmon Tree*. Stephanie spent her early years in New Mexico and Michigan, before choosing Oregon as home. She appreciates birding. To date, she and her husband have recorded 55 bird species in their Portland yard.

MARY SWEIGERT is a writer, runner, mom, digital professional, and amateur pie baker living in Portland, Oregon. Her hobbies include overthinking parenting and dreaming about one day having actual hobbies again.

 **MELODY WILSON** lives in Beaverton, Oregon. She has one Academy of American Poets Award, and several smaller awards including a 2020 Kay Snow Award. Recent work appears in *Windfall, Visions International,* and *West Trade Review*. Upcoming work will be in *Triggerfish Critical Review, Failbetter,* and *Briar Creek Review*.

 **JANET JIAHUI WU** is a nonbinary Hong-Kongese-Chinese-Australian visual artist and writer of poetry and fiction. She has published in various literary magazines big and small. She currently lives in South Australia with two sassy fat cats, Puss (in boots) & Pablo (Neruda). She acknowledges that the land on which she stands belongs to the Kaurna people and pays respects to their Elders past, present, and emerging.

CPSIA information can be obtained
at www.ICGtesting.com
Printed in the USA
FSHW022319160821
84089FS